Leadership by Numbers
for God's people who count

Reverend Alfonso Wyatt, D. Min.

Leadership by Numbers

cover design by Lucy Swerdfeger

Published by

The Power of Hope Press
6137 East Mescal Street
Scottsdale, Arizona 85254-5418

ISBN: 978-1-932842-84-5 — $ 14.95

The Power of Hope Press seeks to publish books drawn from actual life experiences that educate, edify, and inspire.

Printed in the United States of America

Also by Rev. Dr. Alfonso Wyatt and Rev. Ouida C. Wyatt
(available at Amazon.com or Barnes & Noble online)

Soul Be Free Poems Prose Prayers
Soul Be Free II
Mentoring From The Inside Out:
Healing Boys Transforming Men
Before You Jump The Broom, Clean Up Your Room

LEADERSHIP
by Numbers for God's people who count.
6:23-27

Acknowledgments

I thank the all-loving and merciful God for every hill and valley in my life that has shaped my character and journey to this point. I thank you Lord for Evangelist Ouida A. Wyatt, my loving, insightful, and encouraging wife who saw promise in me long before I could see it for myself. Much love to my parents, Pastor Emeritus William Nathaniel Wyatt (deceased) and Pastor Mae Wyatt, co-founders of Friendship Church of Christ Baptist, my siblings Curtis, Lorraine and Deborah, godchildren, mentors, mentees, co-laborers in the Gospel, and learning partners. A special thank you to my spirit son Shawn Dove for his fine example of social entrepreneurship, and push to complete this book. I must acknowledge the peerless example of ministerial leadership of Pastor Floyd H. Flake, D.Min. and Co-Pastor Margaret Elaine McCollins Flake, D.Min. of The Greater Allen A.M.E. Cathedral of New York. Finally, I want to recognize every leader in my life; some of you taught me what to do while others showed me what never to do – and for this, I am grateful.

A special thank you to Reverend Kim Mayner
and Brother Jimmie Briggs...

Preface

This book is written for leaders who may ask, "What in Heaven's name (or the other place) possessed me to be in charge of this ministry?" Have you ever wondered, "Where on earth did these saints ("Aint's") come from and why won't they listen, move on, or, God help me, just die?" Are you haunted by not knowing what should be the next move, the next thought, or the next word in order to take followers to the next level? These questions are not new. Anyone who has decision-making power is a target for second-guessing and headaches caused by recalcitrant followers. If you know that it is hard to lead folks (some may refuse to be led) – rejoice because you are reading the right book, prayerfully, at the right time. If you have prayed for a leadership-breakthrough – your time is nigh.

It has been said that when the student is ready to learn the teacher will appear. If you are ready, the teacher in the person of Moses has arrived. He is widely recognized as one of the great leaders in the Bible. Moses asked the aforementioned questions over a period of 40 years (how long have you been in charge?). He experienced the joy and angst of his calling. He was alternately revered and reviled by the people *he was chosen* to lead. Moses had favor and actually dialogued with God, but he still had nagging leadership questions, doubts, fears, wants, hurts and disappointments. How could this be?

Now that we have these statements and questions on the table, it is time to look for answers contained in the Old Testament's *Book of Numbers*. The Hebrew title for Numbers is bemidbar; it means, "in the desert or wilderness." You may think, "Oh no, not Numbers with the dated religious rituals, endless wandering, long census and horrific battles; Lord, any book but Numbers ('am I projecting?')." Who said leading would be easy? I culled from this fourth book of The Pentateuch (the first five books of the Old Testament) the leadership challenges faced by Moses (including the Balaam narrative) as he guided God's people out of captivity to the land that was promised. Moses was challenged in the form of endless murmuring, grumbling and complaining (a recurring motif in Numbers). Some issues were, "your spirit vs. my spirit; who said you are the only one who can hear from God; good intention/bad result scenarios, and, 'who put YOU in charge of me' confrontations."

Leadership By Numbers: For God's People Who Count, unpacks timeless leadership lessons, people management techniques, understanding of group dynamics, and offers spirit-revealed insight (the best kind) for readers who are, or wish to become effective leaders. I was instructed by the Holy Spirit to research examples from Numbers that highlight God's unmerited favor, inexorable power, faithfulness and triumph over human adversity and opposition. Do not become dismayed when you do not see private sector leadership examples, copious footnotes, or worse, you do not see Jesus' name, or citing from the New Testament. That was all by design.

The focus of this book is on wilderness inspired leadership lessons, the maturation of Moses, and

God's revealed character and promise. There are books that venture deep into the spiritual, psychological and managerial makeup of leaders. I thank God for the accomplished authors who have written about leadership that draw on research and experiences gathered from a variety of sources; however, I was led in a different direction.

Leadership By Numbers presents material in a readable format to help emerging as well as established leaders avoid the spiritual, psychological and managerial pitfalls that have stunted or destroyed ministries, reputations and churches. Some lessons will focus on the leader's relationship to followers (and vice-versa) and decision-making, while other lessons uncover positive and negative personality traits of leaders.

Numbers highlights the multilayered tension between leaders and followers, as well as the battle between spirit and flesh. The chapters chronicle the supernatural development of leaders born into slavery who would later hone skills through their wilderness experience. Numbers depicts the migration of what some scholars say was over 2,000,000 people through inhospitable territory and their bloody encounters. This epic trek, complete with children, elders, the infirmed, disgruntled, detached and fearful, all carrying their meager possessions on beasts of burden, had to be a logistical nightmare. The exodus through the wilderness would be hard to manage today even with the help of IPads, cell phones or GPS, whether one was a CEO, or had an MBA.

The lessons you will read are presented according to Moses' real time encounters referenced in Numbers. Each lesson will contain a framing passage of scripture (NIV unless otherwise noted), a leader focus area contained in the title, a brief contextual reflection, a modern day application and a wrap-up. Some themes may overlap, however, the application and insights will be different. Several pages after each lesson are left blank so readers can jot down notes, ideas, or emerging personal thoughts.

Leadership By Numbers draws upon my four decades of professional experience: managing people; problem-solving; leadership and program development; mentoring and coaching; group facilitation; organizational capacity building; training; writing; reading; along with learning from successes and failures, all wrapped in good 'ole fashion mother wit' (thank you *Mamae*), and a dash of humor. I have been a member of small, mid-sized, and a "mega" church, as well as working in and with various secular institutions. In my role as a pastor to pastors, an honorific given by a fellow clergyperson, I have trained lay and ordained leaders, and served as a role model and mentor to several thousand young people, as well as peers in and out of the faith community.

The study of the many leadership challenges and organizational issues found in Numbers offers a rich array of relevant lessons, case studies and insights through scriptural reflection and storytelling: modes of learning consistent with the ethos of the church. This is important because the church is one of the few environments where leaders are expected to "go forth" and lead, often without an identifiable and/or consistent process of preparation and training.

While "OJT" (On Job Training) has legitimate application in some sacred and secular work titles, OJT should not be the only way leaders are developed. If your house of worship has a process to prepare and assess leaders, this book can still be useful. Having a degree, certificate, or prior supervisory experience does not automatically mean a person is qualified to be a leader in a faith setting.

I have witnessed leaders either take on too many challenges or avoid them all together. I have seen leaders grow or wilt under pressure. I have discovered how leaders can make mistakes based on faulty information, hasty assumptions, or a supreme belief in their ability. I have counseled leaders whose private sins became public. I have seen leaders at their weakest moment, filled with shame, fear or anger. I have witnessed leaders address seemingly insurmountable problems with wisdom, class, creativity and unshakable faith.

It is important to say that no church that engaged my services, or where I currently worship for that matter, serves as the genesis of this book. The case studies you will read are composites drawn from various sacred and secular venues. In my years of Christian membership and leadership, I have learned this truism that different churches and denominations face the same adversary and problems. Please also know that the name of people, their house of worship, or any secular settings are not identified.

Leadership By Numbers: For God's People Who Count can meet different needs and challenges that arise in most sacred settings. It can serve as a compass for leaders seeking direction. It can affirm what is right in the ministry as well as illuminate problem areas. The book takes an unblinking look at the important, and often complicated, interpersonal relationship between leaders and followers. As a former public high school educator, counselor, college and seminary adjunct professor, I am sensitive to varied learning styles of people. With that in mind, the lessons, chapter titles, concepts, case studies and insights can be discussed, journaled, emailed, taught, or preached from the pulpit (with appropriate modification).

Read this book in a manner that is comfortable and productive for you. You can go through *Leadership By Numbers* lesson by lesson, or choose relevant chapters. Use gained information to stimulate internal conversation leading to external evaluation and, ultimately, develop lasting change strategies. Share lessons and insights with people in your spiritual, personal and professional space who count. Last thought, before we start "running the numbers," it would be helpful to keep your Bible at the ready in order to read and examine the full context of each lesson's framing scriptures even if you are familiar with the text. Let us begin our sojourn with Moses.

Leadership By Numbers
Table of Contents

Foreword

By Reverend Andrew Wilkes M.Div.

Reverend Dr. Alfonso Wyatt is an exemplary leader of God's people. By personal experience and firsthand observation, I have seen him pour into the lives of leaders from the Civil Rights, Generation X, and Millennial generations. His life embodies the Jesuit truth that godly leadership is a committed convergence of contemplation and action. As a mentor, motivational speaker, prophetic preacher, social entrepreneur, former foundation executive, and CEO, he is a well-equipped messenger with a well-timed message for this season. Dr. Wyatt is setting the standard for congregational leadership by leaving an intellectual inheritance for the body of Christ. He is a man of God and of letters – encouraging faith leaders to leave a written legacy to complement the sermonic storehouse that will cease when preachers ascend the sacred desk for the last time.

Dr. Wyatt incorporates a multiplier effect into his ministry – by divine providence, his texts teach in places and among audiences that he may never see face-to-face. My prayer is that congregational change agents, of all generations, will heed his example by committing to a ministry of writing. We live in an age where Christian content is increasingly accessed through tablets – iPads, Kindles, and Nooks. Appropriately understanding this "sign of the times" obligates the Church to honor the ministry of composition as a supplement to, and a form of, the ministry of proclamation.

Leadership By Numbers: For God's People Who Count is an incisive intervention into current conversations about practical theology and ministerial practice. A lifetime of hard-earned wisdom is distilled into nineteen lessons on leadership. Throughout his leadership journey, Rev. Dr. Wyatt has been a teachable teacher. In *Leadership By Numbers,* he likewise challenges readers to conduct an inventory of their personal leadership history while appropriating the precepts of each chapter. This text is tailored for its audience: each lesson speaks with equal force to ordained and lay leaders of congregations, parachurch organizations, and other ecclesial groups.

The following lessons are battle-tested dispatches from a leader who thinks critically about shepherding people of faith. As Ronald Heifeitz reminds us, leadership is not about managing people from positions of authority, but mobilizing people to address adaptive challenges. *Leadership By Numbers* empowers readers to exercise adaptive leadership by tackling the tough terrain. Dr. Wyatt offers actionable models for dealing with burnout, managing congregational changes, working with difficult people, nurturing faith in difficult environments, and more. Each lesson achieves proverbial profundity: enough detail to be authentic, enough conceptual heft to apply across differing circumstances and regions.

The chapter on delegation is worth the price of book. Leadership is too great a burden to bear alone. Identifying self-starting, Spirit-led, saints to share the load creates the conditions for "marathon ministry" – teams serving well over time instead of being burned out in no time flat! Through scriptural exposition, example-based reasoning, and a refreshing use of humor, Reverend Wyatt invites readers to walk with him on a journey through the book of Numbers.

I challenge you to read *Leadership By Numbers* multiple times. It is that good. I laughed - and nearly wept – while considering the lesson, "If You Don't Know The Answer, Ask God the Question." Instead of bringing our situational dilemmas to The Lord, Dr. Wyatt perceptively notes that we resort to MSU – making stuff up. Who has not been there? Dr. Wyatt's disarming humor will lead you into a safe space where the four R's of leadership can occur: personal reflection, earnest repentance, spiritual renewal, and a combination of prayerful *and* thoughtful recommitment to the work of inspiring, teaching, and guiding people. Dr. Wyatt's logic is convincing; his exposition, sound; but his humor may be the difference maker for leaders who are afraid to analyze their leadership patterns and paradigms.

For young leaders, Dr. Wyatt offers cautionary wisdom to prevent ministerial missteps at the dawn of an early career. Seasoned leaders will discover prudent models for conflict management and church administration. Legacy leaders: Dr. Wyatt challenges you to "prepare the congregation and a successor" to carry on the good fight of faith and ensure a smooth pastoral transition. Wherever you are in your leadership journey, Dr. Wyatt has a word to help you with the next leg of your sojourn. Grab a journal, get a highlighter, and prepare for a life-changing experience that will strengthen the quality of your leadership.

Rev. Andrew Wilkes is the Executive Director of The Drum Major Institute. Wilkes has built his career on a dual commitment to economic development and economic justice. As a Senior Grants Manager at The American Red Cross, Wilkes oversaw a $45 million budget for Hurricane Sandy recovery in New York State and Connecticut. Before that, Wilkes engaged 140 faith communities as the Faith & Community Relations Associate at Habitat for Humanity NYC. Wilkes currently serves as an Associate Pastor of Social Justice and Young Adults at The Greater Allen A.M.E. Cathedral of New York. He is the 2013 recipient of both Rev. Jesse Jackson's Rainbow Push Advocacy Award, and the 2013 Frances Hesselbein Leadership Institute Next Leader of the Future Award. A graduate of The CORO Public Affairs Fellowship, Princeton Theological Seminary, & Hampton University; Wilkes also writes for The Huffington Post, The Guardian, and other publications. Rev. Wilkes resides in Harlem, NY with his wife, Gabby Cudjoe Wilkes. Follow him on Twitter @andrewjwilkes.

Leader Lesson 1
Are You Too Stressed To Bless?

Numbers 6:22-26

The Lord said to Moses, "Tell Aaron and his sons, This is how you are to bless the Israelites. Say to them: The Lord bless you and keep you; the Lord make his face shine upon you and be gracious to you; the Lord turn his face toward you and give you peace…' "

It is fitting to start our leadership journey the same way the Lord did with Moses in preparation for his sojourn – that is with a blessing. One of the ministerial roles I value is bestowing blessing on babies, individuals, homes, and human endeavors. A blessing is proactively powerful and empowering. A blessing speaks wants into the atmosphere like the needed ingredients for change, or speaks to what is missing but is on the way. A corporate blessing can create a strong sense of togetherness when the sentiment of the words is owned, believed and shared.

The scars of captivity ran deep. Moses and Aaron had to learn how to block out their personal feelings in order to do God's will. The brothers found out that it is easier to bless people when there is love, peace and harmony in the camp. Moses and Aaron had to grow to the point where they could bestow a blessing when the people were stressing.

If being in charge is robbing you of sleep; if you feel paranoid, overly sensitive, your appetite has demonstrably changed, you are suffering hair loss, have had panic attacks, or you just feel on edge all of the time – you are stressed. Our God-designed central nervous system can automatically translate our external cues, stimuli, observations, perceptions and situations into emotion or behavior. When this system is overloaded (stressed), or senses an attack (real or imaginary), it launches into fight, freeze, or flight mode. These primal responses are deeply encoded to protect us from danger. Our bodies were not made to function under stress for an extended period. When this happens, we slow down, run down, or eventually shut down. A stressed-out leader may make decisions based on easing personal discomfort, and not what is best for the situation.

It is not easy to bless folk who bring hidden agendas, pettiness, jealousy, anger, authority issues and personal stuff. We are the products of our life's experiences, the good, bad and ugly. Some folks are able to work out their personal issues, or are willing to take responsibility for their behavior, thereby managing their stress level. We should thank God for people who exhibit this valuable characteristic. However, sisters and brothers who are unaware of the impact of their behavior on others can cause leadership stress leading to confusion, fights, time wasting flights, inefficiency and ultimately burnout. It is hard for a person to change behavior that is not recognized or owned. It is also difficult to see yourself the way others see you.

For example, the person who relishes saying whatever comes to mind, no matter who gets hurt, may see himself as insightful, smarter, or bolder than everyone else. The group may see him as a pompous, arrogant insensitive so-and-so (we are talking about blessings here). Here is the challenge: Some people may not know if their actions lead to stressing or blessing. The easiest self-diagnostic test I know is to ask the questions, Lord is it really me? Am I the one creating confusion? Are my needs overriding the needs of the ministry? Is there something I lack that I am trying to get by being hard to please? It is amazing how one's vision fails when it comes to seeing personal flaws. The inability to connect the dots and see one's self creates a web of tangled intentions that can raise the ministry stress level. A common mistake a stressed-out leader may make is trying to placate the stressor. If you are trying to buy peace by making costly concessions, please know that all you are doing is buying trouble on the installment plan. Be clear – there will always be stressful leadership moments. So how do you handle your stress?

I remember many years ago accepting a leadership position at a public high school when stress got the best of me. I said, "yes" to the offer thinking I would lead the teachers who helped establish the school. We knew the system, worked well together, and were friends. As soon as I moved into my new office, my trusted colleagues, one by one, told me this would be their last year. I inherited new teachers who were largely system "cast-offs" and did not share the "open student engagement" philosophy of the school. These teachers wanted strict interpretation of the rules and complained incessantly. Nothing was ever good enough. I can still close my eyes and see the faces of my stress inducers.

During this time, I remember not sleeping through the night. One way I passed time during the dawn hours was closing my eyes and visualizing the intricate pattern of the cracks on the ceiling. When the express bus I rode to work every day neared my stop, I knew by the knot in my stomach that I was in for more stress. I endured this situation for nearly a year. I worried more than I ate. I eventually left the school system after a citywide layoff. On the way out the door, I prayed, "Lord if I am ever in charge of a workplace again, please help me not create a psychological and stressful work environment that destroys the confidence of workers and essentially makes work Hell." Over the last four decades, I have had supervisory responsibility. Did I like all of my colleagues? No. Did I treat people fairly? I tried. Was it difficult? Yes.

So where does blessing enter into the picture? I recall a leader who had conflict with many people. After one particular encounter, I decided enough was enough. I was hurt and angry and decided to seek retribution. This Word dropped in my spirit and stopped me: "Vengeance is mine, I will repay." I thought, "I don't want a Bible study, I want to get even!" The following evening after most people were gone, I was led by the Lord to bless the desk of my stressor of days. I said to myself, "I ain't doing it," even as I reluctantly walked toward the person's vacant work area. I did not know it then but I prayed a blessing prayer. I did not ask for a supernatural fixing, or a sudden death. I offered a generous string of work and family blessings. I came in the next day and it was apparent that the person had not changed, but after offering this blessing prayer, it was equally apparent that I had changed, and it was for the better.

The tension of escaping slavery, wandering in the wilderness and constantly facing seemingly insurmountable trials and tribulation had to cause stress levels to rise off the charts. The Lord knew what was ahead for Moses. He knew the hearts of the people. He knew His chosen leader was going to be tested. It would seem counterintuitive to bless folk who cause stress to enter your life. Moses had to learn how to fight off the desire to seek revenge or take the 'wilderness low road'. His compassion level had to rise above his stress level. He had to learn how to bless in the midst of mess. Moses had to discover the fundamental premise of a blessing: What goes around comes around so when you bless others, you are also blessing yourself.

Leader Lesson 2
Don't Know the Answer

Ask God The Question

Numbers 9:4a, 6-8

So Moses told the Israelites to celebrate the Passover...
But some of them could not celebrate the Passover on
that day because they were ceremonially unclean on
account of a dead body. So they came to Moses and
Aaron that same day and said to Moses, "We have
become unclean because of a dead body, but why should
we be kept from presenting the LORD'S offering with
the other Israelites at the appointed time?" Moses
answered them saying, "Wait until I find out what The
LORD commands concerning you."

Moses faced a spiritual dilemma. According to the
cleansing ritual found in Leviticus, members were
defiled if they touched a dead body and had to go
through a priest-led process to be rendered
ceremonially clean. The problem facing Moses was
that he was preparing the people for Passover, one of
the highest and holiest days of remembrance and
celebration. Moses could have "followed the rules"
which were clearly delineated and deny the
"offenders" the chance to sit at the Passover table.
We find that he exercises supreme wisdom and
consults God.

Leaders, be prepared for situations that are not black
and white, but endless shades of grey. Black and white
issues can usually be addressed by a "yes" or a "no"

response, but grey issues may call for a "maybe," "perhaps," or "it would seem so" responses. When a leader confronts uncertainty, he or she may feel compelled to make a snap decision, especially when supported by religious tradition, past practice, or a seemingly clear decision. Tradition-driven churches have their own written rules and regulations designed to answer recurring questions and maintain order. This can be a tremendous help, or it can be a spirit/church killing hindrance, depending on how rules are interpreted and/or implemented.

The worst thing to do when faced with a problem and you do not know what to do is resort to "MSU". This is not a university. It is not a new decision-making program. It means *Make Stuff Up*. Leaders, never render an "eeny, meeny, miney, mo" inspired decision to a thorny question. Why do folk give in to MSU when they do cannot figure out what to do? Here are some thoughts based on years of MSU observation and, sadly, MSU participation:

1. The leader does not know the answer to the question and is frantically searching while desperately leading.

2. The leader feels she should have all the answers and does not wish to appear ignorant or incompetent before the group.

3. The leader believes he has found an easy answer to a difficult question and refuses to complicate the problem further by exploring other options.

4. The leader purposefully slants decisions to give special favor to a person or persons in the ministry.

5. The leader is a narcissist; and has made the sad mistake of falling in love with his thoughts.

6. The leader thinks everyone else is incompetent and feels justified making all the hard decisions.

7. The leader believes that she or he is solely and divinely in charge and does not believe in shared decision-making with people who are not as attuned with God.

8. The leader depends too heavily on secular experience and tends to ignore the "spooky" spiritual stuff for guidance.

9. The leader always says, "I'll pray on it," but never gets around to doing it. When pushed, he makes up decisions and says it is from God.

10. The leader is easily intimidated; the fear of looking unprepared is greater than the reality of being unprepared.

These are just a few reasons why some leaders may give in to MSU instead of following God's lead. Please feel free to identify other MSU experiences in the notes section that you may have participated in or have encountered. While we intellectually grasp the fact that it is impossible for a person to know everything, no matter how much education or experience he or she may have, there are questions that beg for answers and situations that defy cookie-cutter approaches.

When leaders confront challenging problems, the person must seek higher counsel from the shepherd of the flock and God. This honors the fact that the shepherd (pastor) receives the vision from the Lord and that vision passes along to chosen leaders to implement. When ministerial decisions cause friction, pain or wasted effort through confusion, these are clear signs that it is time to seek God's counsel (and forgiveness) and not blissfully cling to MSU.

A word of caution, there can be errors on the other side of MSU when a leader petitions God for any and everything. For example, do not call a church-wide fast to discern the color of the anniversary punch, or pray for pattern revelation for the Men's Day pocket squares and matching ties. Bring to God issues that are worthy of God's attention and involvement. Please do not bring decisions you have already made and you seek the Lord's sanctification to justify your situation. This is disrespectful to the office of leadership, the trust bestowed upon you, and makes you guilty of attempted manipulation of God.

Go back to the scripture reference. We are told that members of the community were exposed to a dead body. The text does not tell us the circumstance. The Law is clear regarding what ceremonially unclean means. It called for removal of the offending party from the community in order to go through a ritualistic cleansing process. It would seem that the pleas of the people, under strict interpretation of the Law, would not allow the defiled members to worship during Passover.

Moses presented with a spiritual mind and heart challenge did the following:

- He heard the people's petition and did not make an easy snap decision (MSU).

- He consulted God and got back to the people in a timely manner.

- He did not add his personal interpretation on top of God's decision.

If you read on in the framing text you will discover that God offered a decision that made the seemingly impossible possible. The rendering stated that the people should go through the cleansing process and celebrate Passover a month later. It sounds so simple after the fact. If you do not know, then ask God.

Leader Lesson 3
Effective Leaders Know When To Follow

Numbers 10:29-32

Now Moses said to Hobab son of Reuel the Midianite, Moses' father-in-law, "We are setting out for the place about which the LORD said, 'I will give you.' Come with us and we will treat you well, for the LORD has promised good things to Israel." He answered, "No I will not go; I am going back to my own land and to my own people." But Moses said, "Please do not leave us. You know where we should camp in the desert, and you can be our eyes. If you come with us, we will share with you whatever good things the LORD gives us."

Imagine hearing Moses, the super leader appointed by God, begging his brother-in-law to lead the people through the desert. If Moses is an effective leader, why is he not leading? The simple answer is that leaders do not have all of the answers. Moses recognized that Hobab had desert traveling experience and he wanted the most qualified person to lead. The desert is an unforgiving place. The swirling sands can disorient even the most experienced guide. Moses knew the awesome responsibility of leading his people could not be held hostage by his ego. Some leaders loathe asking for help. When one adds the faith factor, and the need for help, a seemingly discordant image may emerge. One can ask, "If all of my help comes from the Lord, why do I need help from a human being?"

When Moses was called by God to be a leader he offered excuses why he was not up to the task. God finally told him that his brother Aaron would help him lead. Beloved, it is inconceivable to believe it is possible to lead or make it through life without seeking and accepting help from others. Effective leaders are no better than their followers are. It should be clear that just because you are in charge does not always make you right. Leaders can make bad decisions that cause work not to work. An ineffective leader can create as many problems as ineffective followers. Some ineffective leaders are able to disguise their inadequacies and seem on point.

Effective leaders on the other hand earn respect because they know how and when to ask for assistance, direction and feedback. An effective leader believes that there is no substitute for competence. Here are additional characteristics of an effective leader:

- Must discern valid complaints from disguised nonsense.
- Must hold tension of big picture in midst of competing views from others.
- Must consistently align personal and spiritual thought, word and deed.
- Must share credit when successful and see failure as a teacher.
- Must never allow personal smallness to get in the way of spiritual greatness.
- Must be able to motivate others to give the best effort possible.

- Must be an active listener.

- Must not be afraid or too proud to ask for help.

Asking for help is further complicated if chosen sycophants surround the leader. It is sad when a leader selects people who are more interested in keeping their position than getting the job done. A harmful outcome for any leader is followers who will not speak their mind and heart. If trusted supporters think their role is to flatter, protect or ingratiate the leader, trouble can be seen, but may never be reported. A leader should always seek to add skills to the team that he does not possess.

For example, if you are a visionary leader make sure you reach out to a strong implementer or all you will ever do is plan. If you are a "hands off" leader, bring on people who can work unsupervised. Leaders who are not intimidated by skilled followers will increase their overall effectiveness in meeting goals. Some say effective leaders are born; others believe good leaders are developed. It does not matter what you think is the genesis of an effective leader; what I can say is that you will know when you are led by one.

Long before actor Clint Eastwood's "Dirty Harry" character uttered this now famous line, "A man has to know his limitations," Moses showed awareness of this fact. He knew there was nothing wrong with asking for assistance, especially when crossing the desert for the first time.

Leader Lesson 4
Do You Have Leadership Blues?

Numbers 11:10-12, 15a

Moses heard the people of every family wailing, each at the entrance to his tent. The LORD became exceedingly angry, and Moses was troubled. He asked the LORD, "Why have you brought this trouble on your servant? What have I done to displease you that you put the burden of all these people on me? Did I conceive all these people? Did I give them birth? Why do you tell me to carry them in my arms, as a nurse carries an infant to the land you promised on oath to their forefathers? If this is how you are going to treat me, put me to death right now...

The people are complaining long and loud about their steady diet of manna (means "what is this?"). So much so, even God's ears grow tired of the complaints. The wailing from each tent begins to wear on Moses. All He hears are indictments, mixed with anger, stating that it was better to be in bondage and eat well than to be free and eat the bland food that God has miraculously provided. The burden of leadership and the ingratitude of the people (a bad combination) became so heavy that Moses begins to rant and complain before God.

Look at his words. Moses is beyond angry. He does not recognize these people as the same folk he started out leading. The grumbling and complaining of the dissatisfied begins to eat away at Moses' spirit. Can you imagine all of your waking hours consumed by whiners and complainers who feel you are responsible for their plight? The irony is that Moses was called to lead and he is following "orders from headquarters" (I heard that preached years ago).

Moses has a deep case of leadership blues evidenced by his plea to God to kill him before the incessant moaning of the people does the job first. I want to disabuse anyone of the notion that just because you are a chosen leader, the people you lead will never make you sing "Nobody Knows The Trouble I Seen" blues. Being a leader can be injurious to your mental, physical and spiritual health if you are not careful and prayerful. This is further amplified when the people you lead do not want to be led. It is important to recognize and affirm people who want to solve problems as opposed to constantly trying to appease folk anointed to create problems.

Ministries can become debilitated by people who feel their contribution is to regurgitate a litany of what is not right, what you cannot deliver, and why they yearn for the "good ole days" before you took charge. There will be times when you rue saying, "I will lead this ministry with God's help." Any leader – learned or self-taught – from a big church, or a small church, will be tested by followers. Your decisions will be called into question. Your authority will be challenged. The people will murmur and complain before, during and after the fact, because for some folk, it is easier to complain than abstain.

There will be days when the burden of leadership coupled with the lack of appreciation, along with second and third guessing, will make you "wanna holler and throw up both hands." It is easy to believe that complaining made its appearance right after you agreed to take the reins of leadership. There will always be malcontents in and out of the church. There will always be victims and beneficiaries of decisions as well as from indecision.

A leader will not be able to please everyone. Leaders may not always be liked, but should always be respected. Some leaders know that the leadership blues will find you no matter what you do because it really is lonely at the top. There are times when your best intention is met by a bad result. Here is a made up blues song that leaders, young or old, experienced or a neophyte may one-day sing:

Ya called me Lawd
Ya called me to lead
Oh yes ya called
me Lawd
called me to lead
But ever since
I said yes
ta ya Lawd
all I hear
is wants and needs...

Moses heard the cries of countless people day in and day out. They blamed him for their present sorry state. Moses did not take the problem out on the people. He carried his burden to the Lord, stating his position and opposition. He did not negate or sugarcoat his feelings in pious ramblings designed to make himself feel better but did not address the situation. Moses decided to sing his leadership blues to the Lord:

> Why have you brought this trouble on your servant?
> What have I done to displease you…?
> You put the burden of all these people on me
> Did I conceive all these people?
> Did I give them birth?
> Why do you tell me
> to carry them
> in my arms?
> as a nurse…?

Leader Lesson 5
The Art of Delegation

Numbers 11:16-17

The Lord said to Moses: "Bring me 70 of Israel's elders who are known to you as leaders and officials among the people. Have them come to The Tent of Meeting, that they may stand there with you. I will come down and speak with you there, and I will take of the Spirit that is on you and put the Spirit on them. They will help you carry the burden of the people so you will not have to carry it alone..."

In the previous lesson, it was established that a leader who accepts help should not take this action as a sign of weakness or ineffectiveness. God knew that there were other talented individuals in the camp. He told Moses to get 70 leaders recognized by the people as such. While the text does not say these men were from a specific tribe, it is a plausible assumption that different tribes were represented. There are many talented people sitting in the pews and pulpits who feel overlooked while waiting to be "discovered." The word for you is to be patient and read the rest of this lesson.

A smart leader must have strong team members in order to maintain maximum effectiveness. So the question to ask is why some leaders will not delegate? I offer plausible reasons using thoughts emanating from a person who flat out refuses to delegate:

1. If I delegate to someone smarter than me that person will get the credit and eventually take over my position (Insecure).

2. It is easier to do it myself because no one on the team is smarter than me (Ego).

3. I have a hard time sharing authority with others (Selfish).

4. I have to oversee and be responsible for every detail because I cannot afford to let the smallest thing get by me (Micromanager).

5. No one cares about the work as deeply and thoughtfully as I do and would never be willing to make the sacrifices I am prepared to make (Martyr).

6. I really do not know what I am doing and if I give away pieces of my work, I will be found out (Incompetent).

7. Suppose I tell someone else to handle a problem and he messes it up; I will be blamed and be removed from my position (Fearful).

8. God speaks only to me and me alone – that is why I am, and should always be in charge (Delusional).

If a ministry is to grow, leaders must overcome the fear of letting go. A church that started in a house or apartment and now has several hundred members cannot administrate as if it still has a few families worshiping around a kitchen table. The recognition to delegate should coincide with growing needs no longer met by one person. Here are some delegation tips to follow:

- Recognize your 'go to' people; give that person assignments you can ill-afford to have fall between the cracks.

- Do not use delegation as a way to test a person's loyalty/ability, or worse, as a set-up to fail.

- Help people grow by delegating assignments that have a high probability of being successfully completed.

- Know the people you have to check up on *before* delegating. Establish a reconnect time *before* a task is to be completed.

- Reserve tasks for yourself that only you can do. All other assignments should be given out to team members.

- Do not use delegation as a way of getting out of work.

- Celebrate success and learn from failure.

- Get in the habit of saying we did it instead of I did it.

- Evaluate the process after the task is completed. Give praise in public and individual correction in private.

The Lord, in his infinite wisdom, created a pattern for delegation for Moses and for all managers to follow by instituting "The 5 W's of Delegation": "Who?," "What?," "When?," "Where?," and "Why?" This level of specificity ensures that the delegator and staff are on the same page. The Lord knew that Moses needed help so he would not have to sing the leadership blues all night long. Let us diagram The 5 W's of Delegation from the scripture lesson:

Who: *70 Known Elders*
What: *Take The Spirit On You And Put The Spirit On Them*
When: *Immediately If Not Sooner*
Where: *At The Tent Of Meeting*
Why: *So You Won't Have To Carry It [Burden] Alone*

My sisters and brothers you have just been taught the art of delegation by the Lord; now go and delegate likewise.

Notes

Leader Lesson 6
Betrayal: The Most Unkind Cut

Numbers 12: 1-8

Miriam and Aaron began to talk against Moses because of his Cushite [African] wife for he had married a Cushite. "Has the LORD spoken only through Moses?" they asked. "Hasn't he also spoken through us?" And the LORD heard this. (Now Moses was a very humble man, more humble than anyone else on the face of the earth.) At once, the LORD said to Moses, Aaron, and Miriam, "Come out to the Tent of Meeting, all three of you." So the three of them came out. Then the LORD came down in a pillar of cloud; he stood at the entrance of the Tent and summoned Aaron and Miriam. When both of them stepped forward he said, "Listen to my words: "When a prophet of the LORD is among you, I reveal myself to him in visions, I speak to him in dreams. But this is not true of my servant Moses; He is faithful in all my house. With him I speak face to face, clearly and not in riddles; he sees the form of the LORD. Why then were you not afraid to speak against my servant Moses?"

With all of the logistics, complaints and the sheer burden of leadership, Moses can add betrayal by his brother and sister to his list of woes. It is one thing for strangers to set you up. This treacherous act came from family. How much did that hurt? Only a person who has been betrayed can truthfully answer that question. Only a loved one or someone who engenders trust can accomplish betrayal. Moses was undermined, ostensibly because Aaron and Miriam did not like his choice of an African for a wife. This feeling of antagonism toward Zipporah opened the floodgate for Aaron and Miriam to question Moses' decision-making and, by extension, his ability to lead. It is amazing what people think, and disheartening to see what they can do, in the name of God.

The Lord called a meeting and plainly presented the facts to the two offenders. An effective meeting should solve problems; bad meetings create problems (more on that later). One should not confuse having a difference of opinion with being betrayed. It is healthy to offer and receive constructive criticism. If the leader considers this form of critique as an act of betrayal, there are larger problems that must be addressed. The act of leadership betrayal has several key elements: it usually comes as a surprise; it comes from an unexpected source; it hurts long after the act. The first casualty of betrayal is trust. A wounded leader must honestly deal with the pain caused by disloyalty in order to move on and grow.

There is another side to a leader's response to past betrayal; that is the expectation of absolute and unquestioned loyalty. This can be a problem if asking questions is viewed as being disloyal. Disloyalty is saying things behind a person's back that would never be said face-to-face. Disloyalty is undermining a person while appearing to be on his side.

Shakespeare wrote magnificent plays that revolved around betrayal and its tragic aftermath. When I was in high school, I was assigned to recite the entire assassination scene in Julius Caesar. Before Caesar died from multiple stab wounds inflicted by conspiratorial senators, he looked at his dear friend holding a bloody dagger and whispered, "et tu Brute ('and you too Brutus')."

While Moses siblings did not physically assassinate him, his character was assaulted. The tongue can be like a dagger and the inflicted wounds can be just as real. When division threatens the vision, betrayal of some sort cannot be too far off. If you sincerely think the leader above you is in error and you feel you have a rival word from God, please reread the scripture lesson. God is not the author of confusion. The Lord will not give out competing messages. If you cannot speak your mind in love, you have no right to spew hateful words that open the door to dissension.

Moses had to be crushed by his family members' blistering attack on his wife thus undermining his leadership. How did he move past the hurt? I firmly believe that he was able to move on because he knew the mission of God was much bigger than his feelings. No matter how frustrated Moses became with the people, he would invariably ask God to forgive their sins. Aaron and Miriam had to be included in his prayer.

The reflection scripture states that Moses was the most humble man in the world. It is amazing that Miriam and Aaron, two beneficiaries of their brother's benevolence, now attempt to turn his strength into a weakness through betrayal. Perhaps they thought his humility anesthetized him from their treachery.

People constantly mistake kindness for weakness. This sad truism is even more amazing when believers make the same erroneous assessment of people who are called to exemplify kindness and love by virtue of their belief in a transcendent God.

Is past betrayal affecting your present ability to lead effectively? If you have been hurt and now wrap your ache in layers of protective excuses guarded by anger, this will affect your ability to trust and lead. It is time to unpack your pain before the Lord. Ask for healing for yourself, forgiveness for your betrayer, then move on with your life. Moses had to tap into the power of love to forgive his errant family members.

While Moses was forgiving, there was a consequence for betraying him in the form of Miriam's banishment from the community after she was inflicted with leprosy. Some scholars suggest that her participation in the plot against Moses was more egregious than Aaron's involvement; therefore, she suffered a stiffer consequence. The take-away from this lesson is not the question of fairness or unfairness of the sentence, but the reality that betrayal of a called servant of God has dire consequences.

Leader Lesson 7
Whose Report Shall You Believe?

Numbers 13:26-28a, 30-32a

They came back to Moses and Aaron and the whole Israelite community at Kadesh in the desert of Paran. There they reported to them and to the whole assembly and showed them the fruit of the land. They gave Moses this account: "We went into the land to which you sent us, and it does flow with milk and honey! Here is its fruit. But the people who live there are powerful, and the cities are fortified and very large... Then Caleb silenced the people before Moses and said, "We should go up and take possession of the land, for we can certainly do it." But the men who had gone up with him said, "We can't attack those people; they are stronger than we are. And they spread among the Israelites a bad report.

Moses was told by God to send out twelve spies to Canaan. We pick up the account as the twelve return to camp. There were two competing reports. The majority (ten spies) stated that the land was indeed blessed and flowing with milk and honey, but there was a problem. The spies gave a horrific account about inhabitants who were like giants living in fortified cities. The majority added more grist for the mill by saying that the giants behind the great walls would consume their flesh. This report spread throughout the assembly as only poisonous bad news can.

It was at this point that Caleb, whose name is synonymous with being "pit-bull" tough, along with

~ 35 ~

Joshua, shouted, "We can take the land." Moses heard two competing messages. The majority's negative report, rooted in fear, inflamed the passion of the people. The community did not hear Caleb's minority report, rooted in God's sovereignty.

Leaders, at one time or another will face some form of contention when attempting to accomplish most tasks. It should not come as a surprise when a leader faces multiple reports and interpretations of the same issue. If the leader does not demonstratively lead at that time, the people will do the leading. The wresting away of leadership can be done in a seemingly pious way, or in a manner similar to how disagreements are handled on the street. For the sake of learning, let us focus on ways people can undermine leaders by spreading contrary personal views:

- Engage in a campaign of disinformation by refuting or distorting the word of the leader.

- Create a distraction when critical decisions have to be made.

- Withhold, vital information, critical support, or conveniently "forget" to come through in the clutch.

- Create and/or manipulate cliques against the leader or fight factions "loyal" to the leader.

- Use passive/aggressive behavior to keep team members off balance.

- Exhibit childish behavior (pouting/temper tantrums and silent treatment), followed by threats to call the leadership; quit the ministry, church, or fall into outright rebellion.

- Duplicitously invoke God's name in a not-so-veiled effort to promote one's own name.

It is easy to fall into the trap of hearing the thoughts of the majority over the muted voices of the few. It was not enough that the ten spies brought back a bad report; they boldly spread their lack of faith to the rest of the camp. Listen to the underlying tone of the majority: Moses does not know what he is doing. We are being led to our death. Yes, the bounty of the land is plentiful; but can we take it? We need new leadership.

So the question is whose report will you believe? Will you follow the report that offers the path of least resistance even though you know it is the wrong way? Will you heed the report of people whom you wish to please because this group holds power and deep down you are really quite ambitious, or will you believe the report of the Lord? The choice is yours — so are the consequences.

Leader Lesson 8
Anointed, Appointed Yet Still Insecure

Numbers 13: 32b-33

"The land we explored devours those living in it. All the people we saw there are of great size. We saw the Nephilim there... We seemed like grasshoppers in our own eyes and we looked the same to them."

As you just read, Moses sent out leaders from the twelve tribes to scout Canaan. These same leaders saw the mighty move of God on their behalf. They witnessed the interruption of the natural laws of the universe. Yet these called leaders saw great opposition. They were not secure enough in God's promise to believe the unbelievable. This shows it is possible to be anointed, appointed yet still be insecure before God.

I do not know what is worse, following an incompetent leader with an overblown sense of self, or a capable leader who is insecure. The first leader, by definition, is a know-it-all and feels what he does not know is not worth knowing. The insecure person may have the tools to lead but nagging doubts erode the base of their decision-making to the point that it becomes easier to vacillate than to facilitate.

The late comedian Rodney Dangerfield was quoted saying, "If you were a bum before you got famous, you will be a rich bum after becoming famous." Following this thought, if you are insecure before becoming a leader, you will be insecure after becoming a leader. One of the great myths of salvation is that once delivered from sin, one is automatically freed from damage caused by sin. We may deal with leaders and followers who manage the dual feat of being high in the spirit, yet remaining low in self-esteem.

An insecure leader may be either harmless or toxic. There are some notable identifying characteristics of harmless/insecure leaders and toxic/insecure leaders. The following "case studies" are presented as prototypes for discussion.

HARMLESS/INSECURE

The harmless insecure leader is generally the type of person who is nice to all members of the team. She tries hard not to create waves, especially with stronger personalities. The harmless demeanor of the leader in question hides the fact that her decision-making is crafted to minimize problems rather than find solutions. The harmless/insecure leader makes an impact with a small "i." It is difficult for some people to be hard on this type of leader. A secondary benefit of naming a harmless/insecure person to a leadership post is that this person will rarely, if ever, rock the boat; they will not steal the boat; and you hope and pray, will not sink the boat. The harmless/insecure leader wants to go home at the end of the day liked by everyone (an impossible feat to accomplish).

TOXIC/INSECURE

This type of leader thrives on self-made or discovered chaos; the more craziness going on creates an opportunity for the toxic/insecure leader to show off his problem-solving skills. This sad situation is similar to the pyromaniac who starts fires for a distorted (tortured) sense of enjoyment; or worse, to put out the fire he started and thereby become a hero. A toxic/insecure leader is a master of playing people off against each other. Soon, the task takes a subordinate role to what is actually going on. This type of leader sees rivals around every corner. The toxic/insecure leader really believes it is imperative to cut folk at the knees before they become a potent foe and take over. A toxic/insecure leader spreads poison that eventually sickens everyone. This person can be charming when it is helpful because he or she worships their position and power more than worshipping God.

The cure for a harmless or toxic leader is the same – honest spirit-led self-reflection. Most people have 20/20 vision or better when looking at the faults of others, but are virtually blind when looking at self. It is difficult to know how one's personality, harmless or toxic, secure or insecure, may affect others.

I recall drawing the "short straw" when the need arose to check a subordinate who was known to be highly toxic/insecure. I discovered shortly after this person was hired that her 'inner editing machine' was broken. She felt comfortable saying whatever she felt no matter whom her words might hurt, embarrass or offend. I knew the confrontation was not going to be pleasant. It is hard to confront a person who has not asked for an intervention.

I led her to a private place, took a deep breath, and told her, "You remind me of an individual who every morning clothes herself in a coat of invisible thorns. Deep down, you wanted to be hugged, but every time someone gets close, they are pricked and withdraw. The growing number of pricked folk have learned it is better to deal from a safe distance or just avoid the thorns altogether."

This true encounter revealed the insecurity under the coat of thorns. It gave the staff member insight into what others felt presented in a non-judgmental way. Here are thoughts about confronting a person not aware of how their behavior is getting in the way:

1. **Be Current.** Do not refer to actions/behaviors that occurred so far in the past that the person cannot honestly recall.

2. **Be Calm.** Do not use caustic language that cloud the issue rather than clarify the matter at hand.

3. **Be Open.** Listen to the person's perception of events and change your opinion if the situation warrants.

4. **Be Fair.** Separate personal feelings from presenting problem.

5. ***Be Concise.*** Do not ramble or randomly pull large, small or insignificant issues that may pop in your mind.

6. ***Be Invested.*** If you do not have a stake in the outcome, it is best to leave the encounter alone.

7. ***Be Resolved.*** Once the issue has been 'put to bed', and both parties move on, do not continually wake it up.

The point of "The Thorn Story" reveals that there is important inner work that must be done if there is going to be substantial and lasting outward change. If you are waiting for the Lord to make you more likeable, less nasty or more balanced without taking steps in this regard, you will be waiting for a long time. The plight of no insight is a person lacking self-awareness. This is not just a play on words. Do not be afraid to take an inward journey. Do not be dissuaded to bust the rusty locks that seal you away from your true mind, heart and soul. There are toxic issues that contribute to one's ill state of being, affecting the individual, family, community, ministry, and church.

Do not be afraid to ask, "Is it really me?" Is it really me that is the problem? Is it really me causing the confusion? Is it really my spirit that is sour?" The answers to these honest simple questions are the beginning of insight. Whether you are harmless/insecure or toxic/insecure, ask yourself, "Is it really me?" If the answer is "yes," then be prepared to make changes. The church needs leaders who have taken the inward journey, and have grappled with their insecurities and have unleashed faith on their doubts. A leader that leads from a secure sense of self is a leader that is a joy to follow.

I remember many years ago asking God to show me the real me that He sees (do not ask this question if you are afraid to see the real you!). What I saw was myself stripped of the excuses, cover-ups, rationalizations and concessions that I had made throughout the years. I saw my real fears and doubts; brokenness; penchant for procrastination, piled up back burner issues and unfinished projects. I was repulsed by what was still in me. I thought, "Oh my God, this is what you see every day and you still love me?" You may not be able to get rid of all of the "junk in your trunk," but you can make the decision to start unpacking.

Moses was anointed, appointed yet still had insecurities. He was insightful and truthful about his shortcomings. He confessed to God what was already known. All of us have issues we either struggle with or skillfully avoid confronting. No one is perfect; it is God doing the perfecting work. If you are content to not discover your true self, be prepared to remain lost inside of yourself. Talk about a wilderness experience!

Leader Lesson 9
Leadership Tag Is Not A Game

Numbers 14:1-5a

That night all the people of the community raised their voices and wept aloud. All the Israelites grumbled against Moses and Aaron and the whole assembly said to them, "If only we had died in Egypt." Or in this desert! Why is the LORD bringing us to this land only to let us fall by the sword? Our wives and children will be taken as plunder. Wouldn't it be better for us to go back to Egypt?" And they said to each other, "We should choose a leader and go back to Egypt." Then Moses and Aaron fell face down in front of the whole Israelite assembly...

The chosen people, yet again, are whipped into a frenzied state. The word circulating throughout the camp is that their leaders are crazy and will cause certain death. It was said that their wives and children would be taken as plunder for marauding idolaters. If this was not enough, the people felt they should choose new leaders and go back to their oppressors. The stage is set for leadership tag. Leadership tag occurs when the people tag the leader with an accusation, or a task, then scamper away because, now, **You Are It.** When you are it, you alone, must resolve the issue at hand, or better said, the issue in the hand that tagged you.

Some leaders have played this game for a long time and have become proficient at **being it**. Tagged leaders feel that it is their job to resolve all of the *"its"* people stick on them. The burden of leadership becomes overwhelming when one is hit by too many "*its*". Every time a problem is identified and is left for the person in charge to figure out, the leader should hear, ***"tag, you're it."*** Have you ever met people who are anointed to find and present problems? I have tagged these extraordinary problem searchers Ph.D.'s of "Problemology." Leaders must teach followers to not only identify problems, but also bring viable solutions.

This chapter can end right here, but unfortunately, there are leaders who love being tagged. In their mind, this is why they are in charge. The need for a leader to feel needed can create an atmosphere of dependency that is ineffective, infuriating and infantilizing. If being in charge is about ego, then the game of tag is what this person loves to play because he or she craves being *"it."* If being needed is more important than being effective, be prepared to become a grandmaster of leadership tag.

The lessons on Delegation and Leadership Blues should be reviewed if you do not honestly understand why a leader should not want to be tagged with every problem. A leader should strive to encourage competency in others. When a leader heads a skilled team, he or she can feel a sense of confidence not being besieged by problem taggers. This is a good time to stroll down memory lane and point out some other games followers may play that can make it difficult for a leader to lead:

Hide-Go-Seek—Disappearing at crucial times when work has to be completed. A variation of this game occurs when a gifted follower intentionally hides their talents in order to escape being pulled deeper into ministry.

May I—Refuse to exercise independent thinking even when the answer is clear. A variation of this game is delaying asking for permission hoping the problem will move to someone else, or be resolved over time. Then a new round of May I can begin.

Double Dutch—A player imperceptibly turns the rope faster than the leader can jump, or intentionally make the rope go slack so the leader messes up in full view of others.

Johnny-On-The-Pony—Pile all of the heavy issues on the leader's back. When the weight gets too heavy, do not wait, add more weight. When the leader finally topples over, do not feel bad, that is the point of the game.

Dodge Ball—Hurl ideas in rapid succession to show power over the leader. Never be afraid to take a shot – even if it is a cheap shot.

Truth, Dare Consequences—Place leader in a position to guess the answer while trying to decipher the question. The players are always ready with a stiff penalty, or manipulative/tempting consequence, in the event the leader fails.

Moses and Aaron were about to be tagged big time. Frustration in the community was at an all-time high and miserable low. The atmosphere in the camp was negatively charged. Moses and Aaron were tagged with labels that suggested both were insensitive, ignorant and incompetent. Thank God the brothers refused to be "it" as defined by the people. They did not rail against their tormentors. They did not feel sorry for themselves or sing "Can't you see what you are doing to me" leadership blues.

It is one thing for people to play tag with each other, but those in rebellion also tagged God by saying that Moses and Aaron would cause their wives and children to be taken as plunder (as if God would not honor His word). The community projected their fear and anger on their leaders, tagging them with the task of doing something about a situation that existed in their collective and unbelieving minds. One could say that this was the genesis of Mind Games.

Leader Lesson 10
When You Disobey Be Prepared To Pay

Numbers 14: 19-23

"...In accordance with your great love, forgive the sin of these people just as you have pardoned them from the time they left Egypt until now." The LORD replied, "I have forgiven them as you asked. Nevertheless, as surely as I live, and as surely as the glory of the LORD fills the whole earth, not one of the men who saw my glory and the miraculous signs I performed in Egypt and the desert but who disobeyed me and tested me ten times— not one of them will see the land I promised on oath to their forefathers. No one who has treated me with contempt will ever see it..."

Moses loves the people even though the people do not always love him. We find our intrepid leader praying for folk who now threaten to stone him and his brother to death – the ultimate in leadership tag. The people are now outright rejecting God. Their disobedience is an affront to the Lord's authority, yet, there was room for divine forgiveness. However, while God forgave the people's sin of disobedience, it is important to note a penalty for disobedience would be forthcoming. God said in very clear terms, "No one who treats me with contempt will see it [Canaan]." Those under 20 years of age would make it to the land that was promised; the rest would die in the wilderness.

This is a clear message and rebuke of foolish leaders who are in open or secret rebellion against God.

There is a natural tension between the will of God and the will of flesh. Let us take this observation into the church. I am against overnight promotion of congregants who may seem right for a leadership position without any meaningful or observable time on task.

When leaders look on the outward appearance, the person may seem to be a yielded vessel with a willingness to do it God's way. However, what cannot be seen is the fight on the inside – the temptation to do it "my way" (flesh). Individuals from the pulpit to the last seat on the last pew are fighting the aforementioned spirit vs. flesh battle. It is important to wait and see what side has the upper hand before giving out titles.

If a person refuses to obey 'little' rules, it is not a big leap to suspect the same person will have difficulty obeying 'bigger' rules. Unfortunately, some disobedient and headstrong people seem to have an uncanny knack for finding their way into leadership positions. These suspect leaders are good at cloaking their behavior in layers of 'church speak' or their existence is sanctioned (tacitly or overtly) by people who benefit from their rebellion. This is getting deep so please stay with this lesson. If I use the church to satisfy my flesh instead of appealing to God to help me with my flesh, then I am disobedient. If I encourage, or wink at, disobedience in others, I am tearing down the very foundation I am charged with building.

Faith leaders are sometimes caught violating their authority by sleeping with parishioners or engaging in financial shenanigans. When personal malfeasance becomes public knowledge, the church loses credibility. There are people turned off from seeking God, or remaining in church, because of a leader's mess. A disobedient leader will never know how many people he discouraged from seeking God because of his flesh-driven actions. Some insolent leaders manage to stay in position because this unholy practitioner of subterfuge knows how to cut holy corners without destroying the entire garment.

The organizational culture of the church can work in favor of bogus leaders. If there is weakness at the top, there will be strongholds at the bottom. If a pastor or ministry leader is not seen as strong (you can be in control without being controlling), then authority will be usurped in pieces or snatched away all at once. When a person surreptitiously sets self over the leader, a seed of disobedience is planted. This seed will yield a bitter harvest. When disobedient leaders hook up with disobedient followers, a conspiratorial cloak of darkness and sin leaves a stain that is hard to remove.

This blemish will not stay hidden for long. The very nature of this type of mark is to mar every aspect of what is just, pure, good and holy. People in the congregation will begin to whisper. The whispers will get louder until there is an official response, or, God forbid, the whole issue is swept under the rug. This pile can get so high that people begin to trip right out of the church, or refuse to enter.

Moses knew his followers went too far. It is one thing to disobey flesh and blood. It is another thing to disobey God. Moses prayed for the people as he has done throughout the wilderness experience. Unfortunately, some recalcitrant folk play on the mercy of God with impunity. The sin cycle of disobey, repent (act right) then disobey becomes the behavior, especially when the person erroneously sense there is no consequence from God.

Disobedient leaders and followers, please do not get it twisted, you are already paying for your treachery. You are dying in stages. You will never keep what you think you have gained through your duplicity. The nagging reality that you are a spiritual fraud will eventually catch up to you. Your co-conspirators will stay with you as long as there are benefits from your sin. In verse 23a, God speaks his heart about disobedient servants when he declares, "You will not treat me with contempt." Yes, you got out of Egypt. Yes, you are free (or so you think). Yes, you are chosen by God… but you will never see the land that I promised.

I offer this prayer on behalf of disobedient leaders in the church to bring conviction that leads to sincere repentance:

Good and merciful God, free misguided leaders from the tyranny of sin. Speak to dissident leaders and followers who refuse to obey your good and perfect will, and repent, turning from their evil ways. Help your people honestly weigh the cost of disobedience against the eternal consequence of damnation. Merciful Lord, cause a spirit of true reflection leading to this pivotal question: Is my disobedience worth paying for with my soul? Amen.

Leader Lesson 11
Trying To Make Wrong Right

Numbers 14:39B-45

"We have sinned," they said. "We will go up to the place the LORD promised." But Moses said, "Why are you disobeying the LORD'S command?" This will not succeed! Do not go up because the LORD is not with you. You will be defeated by your enemies, for the Amalekites and Canaanites will face you there. Because you have turned away from the LORD, he will not be with you and you will fall by the sword." Nevertheless, in their presumption, they went up toward the high hill country, though neither Moses nor the ark of the LORD'S covenant moved from the camp. The Amalekites and Canaanites who lived in that hill country came down and attacked them and beat them down all the way to Hormah.

Moses has to be beside himself. The core of unbelievers, after hearing God's judgment, now decide to follow Caleb's words to take possession of the land, even after Moses forbid them to do so. He clearly tells the people the Lord was not with them and that they would be defeated. In a vain attempt to take a righteous action after an unrighteous deed (making wrong right), the people disobey Moses and try to take the land on their own. They were decisively routed. Actions borne out of personal desperation will not "force" God to react in a manner not consistent with His character.

Every leader will make mistakes. When a leader errs and then tries to cover up mistakes by empty rationalization or lying, that is going too far in the wrong direction. Spiritually deficient leaders cannot sanctify bad decisions no matter how justified he or she may feel. Simply stated, you cannot change a wrong into a right. God cannot and will not bless mess. Any thought to the contrary, no matter how hooked up it sounds, or the number of proof-texting scriptures presented, wrong is wrong.

The church is vulnerable to unscrupulous double agents working the dark and light side of the aisle. Leaders who do not have the gift of discernment may over rely on words. Anyone, over time, can learn church lingo and thereby obscure their real intentions. That is why it is more beneficial to judge actions rather than words. A person's actions are observable behavior stripped of reasons, excuses and pretense. For example, a person pilfers money from the church coffer and, only when caught, claims it was a loan. If later on, the same person says that God really wants him to keep the money, so he must heed God and not the Trustee Board—he is so very wrong.

If you spread false rumors (lie) about a person you perceive to be a threat or blocking your progression up the church ladder, you are wrong. You cannot use half-truths, or outright lies, to get the powers-that-be to see that you are worthy of promotion. Likewise, a leader who participates in a cover-up to shield a friend or to obtain a 'you owe me' chit should know that what is covered up in the dark will be exposed in the light.

Secret sin, once revealed, has a particular stench that is long lasting. It is not a pretty sight when a leader is forced (no one volunteers) to defend the indefensible. The once fluid words are now jumbled. The carefully constructed façade starts to crumble. Beloved, beware of people who can glibly explain the unexplainable and make you believe it is the best option for all involved.

Moses told the people not to fight the Amalekites and Canaanites. He made it clear that God was not with them. This reality forced Moses to withhold sending The Ark of the Covenant, the symbol of God's presence and favor, into battle. If Moses, in a fit of weakness, made a unilateral decision to send the Ark before the people, say, out of sympathy, he would have been wrong in God's eyes and would suffer for his decision.

God will withhold his favor when unrepentant wrongs become business as usual. A leader must be willing to take full responsibility for thought, word and deed. A bona fide leader must first be true to God, self and others. Abraham Lincoln said, "You can fool all the people some of the time, and some of the people all the time, but you cannot fool all the people all the time." I would add to his astute observation: You can never fool God anytime. If you are wrong… get right!

Leader Lesson 12
Mandated Staff Meeting

Numbers 17: 1-5

The Lord said to Moses, "Speak to the Israelites and get twelve staffs from them, one from the leader of each of their ancestral tribes. Write the name of each man on his staff. On the staff of Levi write Aaron's name, for there must be one staff for the head of each ancestral tribe. Place them in the Tent of Meeting in front of the Testimony where I meet with you. The staff belonging to the man I choose will sprout, and I will rid myself of this constant grumbling against you by the Israelites."

God had to call a 'staff meeting' to end all of the grumbling and complaining. That is what a good meeting can and should do. Moses was instructed to write the name of each tribal leader on a staff and bring it to The Tent of Meeting. God told Moses to say to the community that the staff that buds (which is impossible) is His chosen leader. The next day the people sees that Aaron's staff not only buds, but also produced almonds (beyond impossible).

God called a mandated staff meeting to get things straight. Moses was told to go to the Tent of Meeting before the Testimony (Ark of the Covenant and The Ten Commandments). The meeting showed the community that Aaron, not the followers of Korah, was God's choice for the position of high priest.

Have you attended meetings that generated more troubling questions than answers, in short, a total waste of time and effort? There are concrete reasons why meetings are either effective or ineffective. Here are some ways to foster effective meetings:

- **Shared Agenda/Goal In Mind**—Transparency is important. If ministry members sense a hidden agenda, or attempts to manipulate outcomes/goals, group cohesion will suffer.

- **Stay Focused On The Big Picture**—It is possible to become micro-focused on minutia. Distractions can take a leader and group's eye off the big picture. The insignificant should never be allowed to overshadow the significant.

- **Consistent/Effective Follow-up**—What can be more frustrating than circling the same concerns without resolution? Endless meandering wears down a team's desire to seek viable solutions once it is clear that the group is moving but not going anywhere.

- **Recognize In Public/Chastise In Private**—Unfortunately some leaders reverse this action and use meetings as a platform to chew out and/or intimidate workers. If the general tone of meetings is steeped in hostility, team members will engage in fright or fight – neither mode is helpful in the end.

- **Separate Personal From Professional**—Every leader has feelings and blind spots. Using one's leadership position to make friends, or dole out favors, blurs the personal and professional lines between the leader and followers. This action will create trouble down the line.

- **Start/End On Time (With Prayer On Both Ends)**—Self-explanatory.

Here are some ways to foster ineffective meetings:

- **Call Meetings With Little Or No Notice**—This action contributes to a sense of disorganization. It also can be used as a tactic to make sure the "wrong" people, as defined by the meeting manager, are not present or prepared to meet.

- **Create Lose/Lose Situations**—If fighting to defend one's ego or position is more important than finding viable solutions, then everyone loses.

- **Honor Cliques/Play Favoritism**—When there are harmful intergroup factions, and the vision is threatened by division, meeting efficiency will be lost, as well as the team.

- **Avoid/Ignore Conflict At All Cost**— Conflict is real; ignoring it can create a surreal atmosphere where members find different ways to tiptoe around critical issues. Eventually, the abnormal becomes normal.

- **Consistently Change Definition Of Success**—If a group never feels successful because benchmarks/goals are capriciously changed, a "why bother" attitude will set in.

- **Never Ask How Can Meetings Be Improved**—If you don't want to know, don't ask. All meetings can be improved if the goal is excellence and not maintaining a dissatisfying status "woe."

God called a staff meeting to clearly demonstrate His power and favor by backing Aaron, showing once and for all who was in charge and the consequence suffered by usurpers of His power. This is the height of meeting efficiency when the twin titans of change, namely, cause and effect, are recognized, expected and respected. The result the next day was so clear regarding the visible budding of Aaron's staff that no credible person could argue. If that was not enough, God allowed almonds to come forth on Aaron's staff – out of season, out of the ground and beyond question. Now that was a productive staff meeting!

Leader Lesson 13
Then Accept Responsibility

Numbers 18:1, 5a

The LORD said to Aaron, "You, your sons and your father's family are to bear the responsibility for offenses against the sanctuary and you and your sons alone are to bear responsibility for offenses against the priesthood"... "You are to be responsible for the care of the sanctuary and the altar"...

The Lord tells Aaron in very clear language that he and his sons (Levites) and his sons son's, will be responsible for the care of the sanctuary, the altar, and atoning for the sins of the people. This is one of the highest positions of authority next to the call of Moses. The Lord, exercising infinite wisdom, linked authority with responsibility when He set up the Levites as priests. Authority is having the official power to act in the name of a higher entity, in this case, God. Taking on the role of leader was new to the Israelites. Their previous work experience was being slaves. God groomed and instructed ordinary people entrusted with executing an extraordinary task by delegating authority.

Some leaders love the power and respect that stems from having authority, but stealthily move away from taking responsibility for improper personal behavior, inept decision-making, or creating an unhealthy atmosphere. There are leaders who thrive in self-created chaos to keep the troops moving even if there is no clear destination or goal in mind. It is depressing to work in an 'Alice in Wonderland' like ministry or church where odd occurrences happen and no one seemingly takes notice or responsibility. Authority without responsibility increases work effort, and concomitantly, lowers effectiveness and morale.

When no one takes responsibility, this is akin to flying on a plane with an impaired pilot; everyone wonders why the craft is flying erratically but no one will take responsibility to check the cockpit. It is difficult to accomplish goals in an environment where responsibility freely moves but never rest in one spot. The frustration of meeting, planning, praying and still not getting the results you want or deserve can eventually hobble a ministry and, by extension, devastate a church.

What gets in the way of the execution of authority and responsibility between leaders and followers? Some plausible responses are:

1. **Leader is micromanager**. This person will not relinquish authority in order to maintain absolute control. Micromanagers tell you what to do, how to do it, and will incessantly check to see if the project is coming along as planned. Some micromanagers, out of compulsion, nervousness or fear, may jump in (uninvited) and finish the task. A micromanager will always have a reason for direct intervention, sometimes valid, but most times not.

2. **Leader is alone**. It is possible to be an effective leader in charge of an ineffective

group. In this instance, it may be irresponsible to give away authority. The power that the mantle of authority bestows must be guarded. Leaders must develop and/or insist on competence and then confidence will soon follow.

3. **Leader is unaware.** There are three points of view when looking at ministry. There is the ministry you run, the ministry you think you run, and the ministry God wants you to run. When there is a wide variance between these three realities, the ministry will suffer.

4. **Leader is poor communicator.** It would be a grave mistake to assume that communication is easy. Truth is that many people are careless communicators. Some blocks that impair productive communication are feelings about what is being said; the tone of voice used; a person's past relationship to authority, gender, class, education issues; combative body language, and the inability to listen.

5. **Leader is weak.** Some cunning followers enjoy working for weak leaders because they can "stir the pot" from a safe and unobservable distance. Ministries and churches can be hijacked by people who believe that God has authored the latest coup d'état. The thin line between divine reality and self-delusion is what makes leading in the church different from heading a secular institution even though

both sectors can experience deluded leadership.

6. **Leader is overwhelmed**. If a leader has too many irons in the fire, there is a chance that she or he may place greater implementation responsibility on the team. Being overwhelmed and not asking for help can turn a good decision-maker into a hasty thinker. If a group member is given responsibility beyond their capacity to comply, most likely failure or shifting blame will follow.

7. **Leader is incompetent**. In a perfect world (talk about an oxymoron), all leaders would be competent in the key areas of: managing, directing, coaching/mentoring, assessing, implementing, controlling and evaluating. Since we do not live in a perfect world, it is quite possible for a group to be led by a person who is deficient in some or all of the aforementioned areas.

God was very clear with Aaron and did not hint at what he expected. The Lord gave authority, detailed the expected responsibility, and then gave the consequence if His expectations were not met. It does not get any tighter than this form of communication and management perspective. The Levites, while set apart from the Israelites, were no different from the other tribes. The spiritual needs of the people had to be met by leaders susceptible to the same shortcomings, temptations and hurts as the masses. This carnal/spirit balancing act must be kept in the forefront of a leader's mind if he or she accepts the call and responsibility of doing God's work.

Leader Lesson 14
Leadership As a Gift

Numbers 18:7a

I am giving you the service of the priesthood as a gift...

God wants Aaron and the other Levites to know and appreciate that being called to serve as a leader is a gift. If we deconstruct the text used for this lesson, we find no wasted words that lead to a lack of clarity; "I [God] am giving you the service of the priesthood as a gift." This tells leaders that being called to serve is a gift from The Creator. This should never be misconstrued as a right or privilege given by God's creation. What are you doing with the gift of leadership that God has given to you? It would be great to say that you treasure the gift and treat it with the utmost respect. Unfortunately, human nature being what it is, the gift can be debased, defaced, or destroyed.

Here are some composite "case studies" gleaned over time that illuminate ways the gift of being in charge may be mishandled. The following vignettes are designed to make you laugh, think, stimulate discussion, as well as instruct.

Leadership As A Burden

Sister Tryetou is despondent. The people in the ministry won't act right. There is always a problem, always an issue, always a shifting of blame, frequently, in her direction. Tryetou vows this is the last time she will take on the work of other folk who have the nerve to call her sister. She cannot worship as she did before being placed in charge of The Building Fund Executive Committee. When she sees the hands of her adversaries raised in adoration in the sanctuary, she quickly imagines seeing a firing squad ready to shoot each one of them for their perceived treason. What she initially thought would help the church and provide a lift in the eyes of the congregation through the validation of her abilities has become a tremendous burden. Tryetou feels this ministry will not work after listening to Grandmaster Flash's line from The Message, "Don't push me 'cause I'm close to the edge I'm trying not to lose my head." Her resignation will be emailed to the pastor after service.

Leadership As A Hammer

Brother Harddmanor runs a tight ship. He always means exactly what he says. Some people have accused him of being mean. He sees himself as being effective. After all, the people he is leading are sheep. He refuses to be embarrassed in the eyes of the church shepherd. Harddmanor does not tolerate any free-lancing... ever. He gives written instruction to volunteers and expects absolute compliance. All problems must be routed back to him. Harddmanor works in a secular job that renders him unreachable for large portions of the day. People have to call him at home (which he hates), catch him after church service (which he discourages) or wait until the next staff meeting (which can create more problems). Harddmanor holds himself to a high standard and does not tolerate people who cannot measure up. He makes life particularly difficult for weak people (his term) running behind his back to the pastor to complain about him.

Leadership As A Reward

Sister Touneedey waited a long time for this moment. She is finally the head of a frontline ministry. No more back pew for her; she is right up front where the important people sit. The first thing she is going to do is totally change the ministry personnel and brochure color. All of her friends have been blowing up her cell phone, calling her at home, texting, emailing and all over Facebook, leaving messages about the new ministry openings. They want to know when their hook up will be hooked up. Touneedey knows the people she wants to demote or give a farewell dinner. Most of her friends never served in ministry; they believe people in church get ahead by knowing the "right" people. Touneedey is so excited even though some nosey people are beginning to question why the members who know everything are replaced by people who don't know anything. Touneedey's response is that these malcontents do not know how rewarding it is to be surrounded by like-minded friends in ministry.

Leadership As A Legacy

The Trubloods have been members of the most historic church in town for three generations. Bro. Trublood II is about to retire from work as well as his current church responsibility. He has publicly, and unilaterally, tapped his oldest son to be his replacement. He knows deep down in his heart his son will warm to the idea; after all, he is a Trublood. All that is left to do is to sell Trublood III to the new pastor. There is talk around the church that the pastor-elect (Trublood did not vote for him) wants to institute rotations for all ministry leaders. He even wants to start church-wide training and development workshops for clergy and lay leaders. Trublood knows this rotation idea must fail. He is making moves to sink the pastor's sacred initiative because that would interrupt his succession plan.

Are any of these scenarios familiar? Have you been frustrated, or hurt either by an insensitive, manipulative, or ambitious leader who stepped on, over, or around you? When leadership is not seen as a gift from God anything can happen. Likewise, following a gifted leader can transform a ministry, followers and church. A gifted leader inspires people to reach for the stars together. A gifted leader has a contagious positive spirit that inspires followers. Here are additional qualities of a gifted leader:

- **Strives for consistency**—A gifted leader is not overly moody, therefore it is not necessary to decipher behavioral clues, because for the most part, the same "can do" person shows up each and every day.

- **No big I and little you**—A gifted leader has the ability to make all people feel important not just the ones who already think they are important.

- **Resolves issues rather that allow issues to fester**—A gifted leader strives to be proactive and will not duck hard decisions nor turn molehills into mountains.

- **Sacrifices for the greater good**—A gifted leader will not do what is best for self at the expense of what is best for others.

- **Inspires confidence and trust**—A gifted leader makes the team feel they can achieve great goals by working together. If the team falls short, ministry members are encouraged to learn from what did or did not happen and move on.

- **Can pull the best out of people**—A gifted leader gets the best out of team members not by threats or fear campaigns but through positive expectation, role modeling and prayer.

- **Excellent communicator and listener**—A gifted leader wants to understand and be understood over and above the need of wanting to be proven right.

- **Shares credit and shoulders blame**—A gifted leader takes ownership instead of taking over the "spotlight" when credit is due and disappearing when things go wrong.

- **Exercises mature judgment**—A gifted leader shuns playing mind games or exhibiting childish behavior that encourages people to regress rather than progress.

God expected that the gift He bestowed on the Levites would be valued. Being in charge is much more than being in charge. If the end goal for a leader is to be seen, envied, or feared, this is not a proper way to treat the gift of leadership. The responsibility of handling work related tasks, setting and meeting goals are skills that gifted leaders develop and prayerfully share. The Lord knew that the Levites and leaders to follow must master the following: cooperation, continuity, communication, competence, consistency and compassion in order to be effective in the priesthood. How many C's do you see in your ministry?

Leader Lesson 15
Are You In God's Way?

Numbers 20: 2, 7-11

Now there was no water for the community and the people gathered in opposition to Moses and Aaron... The LORD said to Moses, "Take the staff, and you and your brother gather the assembly together. Speak to that rock before their eyes before their eyes and it will pour out its water. You will bring water out of the rock for the community so they and their livestock can drink. So Moses took the staff from the LORD'S presence, just as he commanded him. He and Aaron gathered the assembly together in front of the rock and Moses said to them, "Listen you rebels, must we bring you water out of the rock?" Then Moses raised his arms and struck the rock twice with his staff. Water gushed out and the community and their livestock drank. But the LORD said to Moses and Aaron, "Because you did not trust in me enough to honor me as holy in the sight of the Israelites, you will not bring this community into the land I give them."

Moses and Aaron are once again the targets of the community's frustration, fear and anger. The people and their livestock need water. It is clear from reading the text that Moses' fatherly persona, patience and humility has worn thin. The years spent wandering in the wilderness, the ceaseless dissension and statements of no confidence in Moses and Aaron nexus at this point. Every person has a testing point that can lead to a breaking point, or turning point. Moses was instructed by God to take his staff and speak to the rock in order to bring forth water. His emotions got in the way. He spoke to the people (calling them rebels) asking, "Must we bring you water out of the rock?" Then he smote the rock two times and water gushed out.

It has been said that the ends justify the means... but not in this case. When Moses positioned himself by implying he could bring water out of the rock, right there is when he got in God's way. Moses and Aaron were not capable of bringing forth water out of anything. Moses was instructed to speak to the rock and water would pour out. There was nothing said about striking the rock with his staff. This was a gross misrepresentation of power evidenced by Moses in the sight of the people.

True confession time, I had trouble with this passage when I first started reading the Old Testament many years ago. I thought it was petty and mean of God not to allow Moses to finish the epic journey because of one mistake. Maturity and careful study of the text helped me to see what really happened. Moses got in the way of God by not giving Him glory and ignoring specific instructions. In the fullness of time (I always liked this expression) I can see the depth of the offense and the teaching opportunity. Our human frailties can get in the way of leading God's people in a manner that is inconsistent with the will of God.

Sometimes the last person to know he or she is out of God's will and is now in God's way is the errant leader. How can this happen? This is the right question; here are some plausible thoughts:

- *Deep In Shallow Water*—Leader is in over his head. I recall talking to my wife about a work related situation and her succinct analysis was that the person in question was deep in shallow water, thus crystallizing the dilemma I struggled to find words to define. There are leaders in the church who feel they are ready for the deep plunge but in reality should stay at the shallow end of the pool and learn how to wade in the water.

- *Spirit/Flesh Tension*—Leader is spiritually immature. It is impossible not to take your flesh issues to church or work, but it is quite possible to leave your spirit at home. If the flesh moves before God's Spirit, there is a high degree that the leader's will is being done and not God's will. As mentioned several times, when a leader's will becomes more important (satisfying) than the will of God, trouble is on the way.

- *One Trick Pony*—Leader is gifted in one area. When it is time for other gifts to be used ministerial effectiveness suffers. A significant amount of time may pass before the church leaders, dazzled by the awesomeness of the one gift, realize that that stagnation has replaced elevation.

- *Hidden Agenda*—Leader is not transparent. The ministry is really a tool to accomplish personal goals. When a person's hidden agenda surfaces, it rarely has anything to do with God's open agenda. A hidden agenda artist has to be sneaky because in order to spring a surprise, timing is everything.

- *Inner Me or Enemy*—Leader is incapable of self-reflection. The inability to see self as a stumbling block. It is commonplace for this type of leader to find fault in others or blame invisible forces and powers for every glitch, problem or failure. It is easier to invent enemies, or make excuses, than it is to take personal responsibility, especially when things go wrong.

- *Church Superstar Syndrome*—Leader is enamored by church fame. Once again my wife coined a term 'lime' disease, not the ailment caused by deer ticks but an acute manifestation of self-grandeur and promotion consistent with narcissistic seekers of the limelight at all cost. This leader wants to be seen, affirmed, and, I daresay, envied by peers more so than being seen and affirmed by God.

- *Hurry Up And Wait*—Leader is moving too fast. The old folks use to say, "You can't hurry God." That has not stopped some people from trying. Life is a process. Most things in life and in the Spirit realm take time. If a leader tries to hurry God by attempting to perceive where God is headed, and try to get there first, mistakes will be made. No one knows the mind of God. Hurry up and wait may seem contradictory. If you agree, stay right here, hurry up and wait, then reread this lesson.

Moses was a great leader, but even great leaders make mistakes. His anger and frustration boiled over at a strategic moment that called for a different response. We are human beings and the rivalry between flesh and spirit will never end. It is important to own your behavior – the good, bad, indifferent, and yes, even the ugly. The Spirit that led Moses out of Egypt and through the wilderness to the doorstep of Canaan is the same Spirit that can guide present day leaders. Covenant to move self out of God's way in order to truly be in God's way.

Leader Lesson 16
What Trouble Can Teach Leaders

Numbers 20: 1, 16b-18

Moses sent messengers from Kadesh to the King of Edom saying..."*Now we are here at Kadesh, a town on the edge of your territory. Please let us pass through your country. We will not go through any field or vineyard, or drink water from any well. We will travel along the king's highway and not turn to the right or to the left until we have passed through your territory.*" *But Edom answered:* "*You may not pass through here; if you try, we will march out and attack you with the sword*"...

Moses has brought the community to the doorstep of the land promised at a desert oasis called Kadesh-Barnea. The quickest route is straight through Kadesh. There is a problem. The Edomites, (cousins to Israelites through Esau) refuse to let Moses and his followers pass through their land. Moses clearly and patiently lays out his case. The Edomites, perhaps wanting payback for the Jacob/Esau birthright fiasco, steadfastly refuse to help. In fact, the army of Edom has been mustered and ready to attack if the Israelites fail to turn away.

There are crucial times when leaders must be firmly and visibly in charge. We have talked about leaders as followers and that is important. It is also important for a leader to know when to be out front when challenging moments must be effectively challenged. If a leader fails to lead in crucial times, informal leadership may emerge from within. Usurping authority may not always be problematic if the action of followers leads to positive results. However, this same act can cause problems by tearing apart group cohesiveness if the takeover is led by a divisive, power-hungry person or faction.

One may think because he or she is engaged in Kingdom building, that opposition can be easily avoided, or defeated. This is patently untrue. Effective leaders should always have a Plan B. There is nothing wrong with having a "what if" contingency plan because it is not always possible to predict the reaction to an action. Do not take "what if" questions as a lack of faith or a challenge to leadership. These probing questions (within reason mind you) can help leaders when constructively offered.

It is impossible to see every possibility or glitch in a plan. That is why it is good business to ask the right questions to the right people. There are individuals who are concrete thinkers who can help deal with emerging issues and interpret secondary consequences. It is important to know problem solvers vs. problem makers. If you go to the wrong person or camp for help at a crucial time, you and everyone else in the ministry will soon discover that a mistake was made.

It has been said that trouble can be a great teacher. It is the mistakes, misjudgments hurts and pains; the good intention/bad results that form memorable positive or negative life lessons. Trouble has a way of focusing attention on the right issue that must be resolved. Trouble does not allow for time wasting distraction (pettiness, he said/she said drama etc…). Trouble will shine the brightest light on an individual's or group's weakest area. Trouble has the power to expose the real you stripped of excuses.

If a situation is determined to be a crisis, business as usual cannot be the first response. Imagine a person violently choking at the family dinner table and no one lifts a finger to help. Perhaps the father thought the mother was supposed to intervene. Maybe the mother thought her other son would make the first move. The reality is that a fixable problem was allowed to become a tragic mistake, complete with reactive excuses, foot-dragging and finger pointing.

Real leaders do not duck or defer the hard decisions that must be made in times of crisis. This is not the time for showing favoritism or trying to appease all factions. It is nice when time affords parliamentary decision-making process, but I assure you this luxury will not always be the case. To be fair, most decisions people make at home, on the job or at church might be important but are not urgent. Learning to differentiate between what is important but not urgent from what is urgent and important can help a ministry prioritize decision-making.

The mundane, trite, or everyday occurrences should never be elevated to emergency status. Do not call an emergency meeting to find out if another meeting is necessary to address a relatively unimportant issue. If people are constantly rousted to address minutiae, it is safe to say, that one day a real emergency will be ignored or mishandled. Trouble and people go together. There are people who find themselves in trouble and there are individuals who create trouble, woe to followers who are led by a person who cannot tell the difference.

There is a mental disorder called Munchausen by proxy syndrome. This is when a parent (caregiver) intentionally makes their child sick then rushes to hospital to orchestrate a dramatic rescue. The point of the disorder is to focus attention, not on the child, but on the anguished parent/adult. Most people will concur that this is aberrant behavior. The same people may dismiss the behavior of a leader that makes a mess of ministry, calls an emergency meeting to clean up the mess and then launches an inquiry into who created the mess in the first place (this is the central plot of *The Caine Mutiny* starring Humphrey Bogart).

Moses and his followers were in trouble. They were under threat of retaliation by the Edomites as safe passage was denied. Moses tried to negotiate but his attempt was rebuffed. The land flowing with milk and honey was within a stone's throw, but it may have well been a million miles away. All of the sacrifices, all of the tears, all of the prayers, now seem for naught. There will come a time in ministry when an incident will rivet and galvanize people to act. At this tense point for Moses, we do not hear any grumbling and complaining. We do not hear from insurgents within the ranks clamoring for leadership change. Trouble has a way of allowing opposition to get folk into position. You have to go through something serious to understand that while trouble is never embraced, it has a way of making people in trouble embrace.

Notes

Leader Lesson 17
Good Fighting Good Is Never Good

Numbers 22: 10-12
(Balaam Narrative)

Balaam said to God, "Balak, son of Zippor, king of Moab, sent me this message: 'A people that has come out of Egypt covers the face of the land, Now come and put a curse on them for me. Perhaps then I will be able to fight them and drive them away.' " But God said to Balaam, "Do not go with them [Balak's emissaries]. You must not put a curse on those people because they are blessed."

This inserted narrative in Numbers turns away from the struggles of the Israelite community. Chapters 22-24 explore how the indigenous people living near and in Canaan are dealing with the inexorable advance of their enemy. Some writers have stated that the Balaam narrative is fictional and/or borrows from folklore from surrounding cultures. It is not my intention to dispute or affirm this claim. There is, however, a powerful lesson for God's people to hear. Balak, the king of Moab, has asked Balaam to put a curse on the Israelites. Balak has witnessed how these 'marauders' were able to defeat the more powerful Amorites on their way through Moab to Canaan. He is worried the same will happen to his people.

While Balaam is a cult prophet acquainted with pagan rituals, soothsaying and divination, he appeals to God and surprisingly receives a response. He is told to leave the people led by Moses alone because the people are blessed, and by extension, whomever God blesses, no man or woman can curse. Balaam was a pagan so God never uses his covenant name with him throughout the scriptural cycle thus indicating the separation between what is Holy and what is not. Balaam, perhaps, thinks that he is communing with another familiar spirit – a small "g" god. He is not fully aware of the power he has tapped.

Deeper into the account we find that Balaam and Balak are at odds because instead of Balaam delivering a curse, he resorts to blessing the people in a series of four oracles. Balaam wanted to do what was good in the sight of God, but Balak had an investment in doing evil. The king offered wealth beyond measure to Balaam as an incentive. Be clear, Balaam wanted the money, but felt compelled to follow God's orders. He wanted to do what was good in the sight of God yet was tempted to do evil against the invaders. God used Balaam despite his pagan beliefs, because He knows that good fighting good is never good. It is time to unpack this truism and see the modern application for leaders.

As a "public theologian," a term former President of Morehouse College, Dr. Robert Franklin, defined for me years ago, I have traveled the length and breadth of this nation bringing a spirit-filled message of hope and persistence to secular audiences. The Lord told me to be light wherever sent. I remember meditating before delivering a speech to a large group of people in the Midwest when this life-changing thought entered my being. I must confess that initially I rejected the premise I am about to tell you because I did not know the lesson came from God. Please hear the words given to me that I humbly offer to you:

You can learn a lot from evil because evil never fights evil in order to do evil. Evil finds ways to get with evil so that evil can go forth united and strong. Look at crack and heroin. If they took on human form, do you think they would argue and fight with each other? Would crack get mad at heroin because it messed up the lives of more people? No, they would scheme and encourage each other in order to fulfill their mission to kill, rob and destroy. Their conversation would sound something like this: "Hey, hey heroin, you jump on these 'wratched' people and slow them down. When I get finished with them, they will find out why they call me crack. I will crack their hope, crack their dreams, crack their spirit and crack their world into unrecognizable pieces." Evil works with evil in order to do evil.

On the other hand, good fights good when doing good. Good argues with good; good sets up good; good tries to destroy good in a vain attempt to do good. Good divides good and feels good doing it. Good minimizes good because it may not look like good. Good will grab good, turn it upside down, and shake all of the goodness out then smugly say to the fragments on the floor, 'Now that's good!'

There you have it, beloved, one of the most powerful lessons conveyed to me. Think about ways that evil sides with evil in order to do evil throughout history. During the Civil Rights Era, segregationist did not argue over how to destroy the hope, dreams, and souls of black folk. They did whatever they could by denying equal education for black children, the right to vote, cheated, belittled, and sometimes, killed black men, disgraced black women and waged a campaign of relentless terror (KKK). Even the courts of the land became co-conspirators with evil by acquitting the obviously guilty who oppressed and killed innocent people.

We who profess to do good will fight one another in order to advance our version of good. When good fights good, the only casualty is good. Good dies an ignominious death and evil stands on the sidelines cheering and encouraging otherwise good people to continue killing good, stomping good, bashing good, ridiculing good, lying on good, thus thwarting good from doing good.

This is an abomination in the sight of God when people called to do good are doing goodness in and still think they are doing God a favor. The question is how do erstwhile good people take on the mission to destroy, hurt, halt or disparage the efforts of other good people? Here are some thoughts regarding how good may feel justified attacking good:

> **Blind Ambition**: This person is intent to rise to the top no matter what or who gets in the way. If people get hurt, the feeling is they should build a bridge and get over it.

> **Social Darwinism:** This person believes that only the strong survive. Their perspective is that the world is divided between sharks and tuna – you are either the hunted or the hunter.

If you come up weak either stay home or quit the team.

I-"itis" Syndrome: This person is wired to look out for self-interest through flagrant acts of self-importance. Victims of I-"itis" refuse to see anyone else's point of view, or need, no matter how clearly presented.

No R.E.S.P.E.C.T.: This person probably did not receive respect while growing up; now as an adult, cannot give respect but will always demand respect.

Holier Than Thou; This person feels empowered to teach other people how to walk on water if only they had more faith. Unfortunately, no one, not even the assigned shepherd of the flock, measures up to their capricious standard and therefore is doomed to sink.

Praying Ceiling Prayers: This person has been praying to God for the right answer to a big problem. Nothing will be said, no action taken, no other thoughts entertained, until there is a divine confluence between the Spirit realm that *happens to coincide* with what is in the person's heart.

The prevalence and ferocity of good fighting good is astounding when you look with supernatural sight. Human emotions can be a friend or enemy to a leader. For example, if you have an adverse reaction to a person, it could cloud future interactions. The object of scorn can have sound ideas that are soundly rejected because of the animus that exist. It should be clear that there will always be some form of conflict when making decisions, even among people called to advance the greater good. Here are some ways to minimize friction that can occur when good rubs good the wrong way:

Hard On Issues, Soft On People: You can deconstruct issues without deconstructing people. It is okay to say that an idea will not work. It is not okay to slander the person who came up with the idea. In short, attack problems and not people.

Good vs. Bad Communication: Loaded communication can increase conflict that drive people apart. Bad communication is rooted in fault-finding, coercion, judgmental language and out-and-out deception. Good communication stems from open neutral language (with I statements – I feel... I would like... I am... etc.), with no blaming or judging.

Look For Win/Win: Win/Win situations occur when disputing parties opt to compromise and walk away with something – perhaps not the whole pie but a nice slice nonetheless. Win/Lose or worse Lose/Lose situations drive opposing sides further apart, increases tension and arms combatants for the next battle.

Agree To Disagree: Sometimes it is not possible to come to an agreement. Disputing parties must recognize differences and move forward. The key to making "agree to disagree" work is when people in opposition endeavor not to be torn apart over differences. Creating a positive, trusting and respectful atmosphere where people give and receive the benefit of doubt is worth its weight in 'good' gold.

Don't Be A Wronged Historian: If you keep painful bitter memories of every perceived wrong and feel encouraged to act out when new situations remind you of old situations, you are a wronged historian. It is fine to learn from the past but it is problematic to use past slights as ammunition for future fights.

Resolve To Resolve: There are people who do not want resolution and will keep messes alive because it is more important to be right than to appear wrong. The necessary condition for compromise is that both sides are invested in meeting each other in the "middle of the room" and be resolved to resolve differences.

God told Balaam not to curse His people because they were blessed. The Lord intervened and did not allow the good Balaam to be subverted by listening to the evil Balak and do what he wanted him to do against Moses and his people. In essence, good was not allowed to fight good. It is time for God's people to recognize that blessed people can differ in opinion from other blessed people, but that is not a reason to resort to vindictive behavior. Leaders do not fight it out when differences arise—they resolve to work it out the best way possible.

I wrote this poem in the early 80's. I see, in retrospect, that I was being prepared for a greater work…

enlightenment

children of the
light
heed this
urgent call
use thine power
o'er darkness
stumble
never fall
illum dark corners
in all
hearts and minds
share this
precious flame
the tie
that binds
hatred is thine
enemy
ignorance
another foe
so band together
small flames
wherever ye
may go
there is strength
in number
remember
ye are light
and every flicker
a wound
to darkness
this
our
eternal
fight

Excerpt from *Soul Be Free Poems Prose Prayers* By Alfonso & Ouida Wyatt

Notes

Leader Lesson 18
Do The Right Thing

Numbers 27:1-8

The daughters of Zelophehad son of Hepher, the son of Gilead, the son of Makir, the son of Manasseh, belonged to the clan of Manasseh son of Joseph. The names of the daughters were Mahlah, Noah, Hoglah, Milcah and Tirzah. They approached the entrance of the Tent of Meeting and stood before Moses, Eleazar the priest, the leaders and the whole assembly and said, "Our father died in the desert. He was not among Korah's followers, who banded together against the LORD, but he died for his own sin and left no sons. Why should our father's name disappear from his clan because he had no son? Give us property among our father's relatives. So Moses brought their case before the LORD and the Lord said to him, "What Zelophehad's daughters are saying is right. You must certainly give them property as an inheritance among their father's relatives and turn their father's inheritance over to them. "Say to the Israelites, 'If a man dies and leaves no son, turn his inheritance over to his daughter.' "

Moses is presented with a problem that has little to do with past challenges. The daughters of Zelophehad argue to Moses, Eleazar, and the entire community, that since their recently deceased father had no son they should be first in line for his inheritance. This was a courageous and unprecedented act because women, according to The Law at the time, were not entitled to any inheritance claims. Can you imagine the five sisters petitioning the authorities (all males) for something that had never been given to females?

Once again, Moses did not Make Stuff Up (Remember MSU?). He petitioned God and was told, "Do The Right Thing."

The decision given to Moses changed the law on inheritance and made women next in line if a father dies and had no son. Sometimes doing the right thing can seem like the wrong thing, especially when tradition, and I add parenthetically, women, are concerned. Moses lived in a patriarchal period were men derived most, if not all the benefits over women. Some would say that there has been little change. It is clear in some houses of worship that denominational interpretation or an individual's preference regarding the role of women in leadership follows a patriarchic model.

I can say, judging from God's decision in the case of The Daughters of Zelophehad vs. Tradition, that God, in His judgeship role, rendered a righteous "Do The Right Thing" decision. The Lord does not have a gender-based standard to evaluate leaders. There is no one set of "blue" rules for males and one set of "pink" rules for females. It is imperative that all called leaders, male or female, adhere to doing the right thing in the eyes of the Lord. This issue was not settled in The People's Court, but was handled in The Court of God.

Here are some additional tips that can help a leader do the right thing:

Stay On The High Road—Avoid the easy and well-traveled trip down the low road's slippery slope. The bottom dwelling folk enjoy trapping unsuspecting travelers in roadside muck and mire conversations, situations and accusations. If someone wants to drag you down this road, fight to turn around, head back up the hill, even if you have to go it alone.

Master Seeing Beyond Looking—Seeing and looking involves the same process but one goes further than the other does. It takes time and discipline to learn the skill how to stop looking at problems and start seeing solutions. A good way to develop this skill is asking, "Can I *see* a lasting solution to the problem that I have been desperately *looking* to solve?"

Always Pray, Never Prey—One letter separates these two words so please don't 'e' when you should 'a'. When leaders use power to overpower folk, mess with their minds, or make sport out them for their own entertainment, that is wrong. Prayer does change things as we read earlier. When you pray a blessing prayer, you are included in the benefits. What goes around really does come around. Do you want to see an 'a', or an 'e' coming after you?

Feed Opportunities, Starve Problems— Some leaders and followers, unfortunately, feel it is their job to feed problems and starve opportunities. Problems are really opportunities in disguise. If you chip away problem's façade, through hard work, analysis, trial and error, the opportunity will eventually be revealed.

Say What You Mean/Mean What You Say—It is frustrating dealing with a person who selectively forgets words uttered days, hours, minutes or even seconds ago. When words lose meaning, then actions will follow suit. Stand by your word. Be big enough to make amends by saying I am sorry if a situation calls for this action.

Separate Personal From Ministerial—If you want to be 'down' with the people and think it not necessary to erect leader/follower boundaries, be prepared to be one of the people. If something off-putting is said while hanging out, or you are placed in a compromising situation, it is hard to jump back into your ministerial leader role to present what thus 'saith' the Lord.

Know When To Get Rest—Though you love the work you do, getting rest means doing something that brings comfort and rejuvenation to mind, body and spirit. If you are rundown and feel you cannot stand to hear another problem or have strength to pick up the phone, send another text, email, or see another person...You Need Rest.

Moses could not take it upon himself to twist the word of God as it related to the situation presented by The Daughters of Zelophehad, even if he personally felt that God's decree was against everything he believed vis-à-vis the role of women. Moses, as God's handpicked leader, had to do the right thing. God is in the business of doing what is right in His sight and not what is right in our sight. If leaders consciously refuse to do the right thing for whatever reason, please know you will never be right in the sight of God.

Leader Lesson 19
Birthing Leaders

Numbers 27:15--23

Moses said to the LORD, "May the Lord, the God of the spirits of all mankind appoint a man over this community to go out and come in before them, one who will lead them out and bring them in, so the LORD'S people will not be like sheep without a shepherd. So the LORD said to Moses, "Take Joshua, son of Nun, a man in whom is the spirit, and lay your hand on him. Have him stand before Eleazar the priest and the entire assembly and commission him in their presence. Give him some of your authority so the whole Israelite community will obey him. He is to stand before Eleazar the priest, who will obtain decisions for him by inquiring of the Urim before the LORD. At his command he and the entire community of the Israelites will go out, and at his command they will come in." Moses did as the Lord commanded him. He took Joshua and had him stand before Eleazar the priest and the whole assembly. Then he laid his hands on him and commissioned him, as the LORD instructed through Moses.

Moses knows his time as leader is coming to an end. He petitions God for help finding his successor. He was instructed to start the dual process of naming and preparing the people for the next leader (leadership succession and congregational preparation are often not linked). Moses is instructed to name and present Joshua to the entire community. Eleazar, the son of Aaron, will anoint him. In this stunning account, we see the model for establishing leadership succession. The work of the Lord must never be held hostage to the time a leader lives. Moses was told that he would not lead the people into Canaan. Does this mean that God's word would return void; or the people got this far but would not be allowed to journey any further?

There is a divine plan that human eyes cannot see but human beings must carry out. That is precisely why God is in the business of birthing leaders. A leader who is not grooming his or her replacement is essentially saying I am going to be a leader forever. This is foolish. Some leaders hold on to their position far too long. Do not interpret this statement as an attack on elders in leadership (I would be attacking myself). What should be heard is that the strength of the church is its ability to pick, prepare and promote new leaders. It is disheartening to see so many diminished ministries and, by extension, houses of worship, that could not survive the illness or death of a leader who refused to plan. Any church with an empty pulpit, no viable candidates (or too many), can attest to this fact. It is the job of responsible leaders to develop leaders; this should be written in a pastor's job description.

A leader's true legacy is predicated on what survives after he or she moves on, steps down, retires, or dies. The measure of effectiveness for any leader is for the work of ministry to continue and thrive. One could argue that leadership succession is a no-brainer. My response is that overlooking simple things can give birth to complicated things. Sadly, this occurs day in and day out in houses of worship, of all sizes and denominations, as one witnesses the growing number of churches with empty pulpits searching for candidates.

Past lessons talked about how followers can fill a leadership vacuum. It has been my observation that the longer congregants, duly constituted or not, run the church, the harder it is to give back power to a new pastor (even if the candidate was the majority choice). This unhealthy dynamic can stunt and divide a church causing a lose/lose dynamic between pastor and congregation that is unacceptable, yet, all too predictable.

If you are a pastor of a church and you are of age to retire, or you are in bad health, you are not serving the people well by not grooming your replacement. I have lived long enough to think about what I want to leave as recognition of my work after I die (this book is part of my desired legacy). It is not a morbid thought, but one that may follow receiving a series of membership applications from AARP. If AARP does not ring a bell then you most likely have time before thinking about your successor. If you prayerfully and honestly deem you have more years in leadership, take time and look over all the ministries of the church to see if this is also the case.

The question still on the table is why do caring, spirit-filled, chosen vessels either overlook or flat out refuse to mentor or name a successor? The easy and complicated answer is, only God knows. However, if I would venture a guess, I would say that fear is a contributing factor. Allow me to project what the voice of fear may be saying to an aging leader reluctant to name a successor:

- As soon as you name the new person to take over you will die.

- Satan is behind this replacement talk so pray and fight until the end.

- What will you do with your life after someone else takes over?

- The people you nurtured and protected need you now more than ever.

- You are not that sick; you have bounced back in the past.

- Making this decision really means you are done.

- Your church members and family will start to pity you.

- It may be the right decision but it is truly the wrong time.

- You looked all over and can't find a suitable replacement.

- Your legacy is in danger so work on it some more.

- Only a few people want you to leave, you should not let them win.

- You do not know concretely if or when God told you to step down.

- Young folk have no respect for tradition so how can they lead.

- You started this church from scratch, sacrificed so much, you should be around to reap the rewards.

- It cannot be over.

Moses did as the LORD commanded him. He took Joshua and had him stand before Eleazar the priest and the whole assembly. Then he laid his hands on him and commissioned him as the LORD instructed through Moses.
Numbers 27:22-23

Conclusion

Moses still speaks to present day leaders in a clear, commanding and relevant voice. His epic challenges reduced to a common denominator, is the reality that personal human smallness will always try to override God's promised gift of spiritual greatness. This is the ongoing tension evidenced throughout this book that all leaders must confront. It is easy to believe that one's education, personal pedigree, relationships with the powers-that-be, or with God, for that matter, will automatically cancel out the work of the flesh. This is not true.

It is incumbent upon leaders to become more vigilant, more introspective and more prayerful when used by God to affect an agenda greater than self. I will go further and say if the adversary does not frustrate you in life and ministry it is because you are not a threat to the "ungod's" domain. As I think about the lessons contained in this book, it is clear that I was led through the wilderness with Moses to extract pivotal lessons that speak to leaders called for a time such as this.

I hope you were able to find yourself in the wilderness. Please know that you do not have to wander, wonder, slander, grumble, or complain. Moreover, it is my solemn prayer that you were able to identify and eliminate any divisive practices; jumbled thoughts; harmful, personal strongholds; stumbling blocks, doubts, character flaws; bad habits; harmful words; or dubious deeds that lessen God in you.

Now it is time to start connecting some of the numbers you have read – because you do count! Moses had no problem sharing authority (Leader Lessons 4 and 5). The insecure leader (Lesson 8) on the other hand sees any suggestion of sharing power or mentoring as an affront. This is not the way to lead. This is a way to fail. The Lord knew that new leadership would have to emerge. Moses was gifted in bringing people out of bondage (counselor / conciliator). If you read on in the Pentateuch (remember?), you will notice the emergence of Joshua who was anointed and appointed to bring people into the land that was promised (warrior/strategist).

Leadership is not a birthright but it is a precious gift to be shared and not hoarded (Leader Lesson 13). Every leader has gifts and talents, strengths and weaknesses. Every leader will have setbacks or can grow weary under the strain of being in charge (Leader Lesson 4). Leaders will make some mistakes and prayerfully learn from their errors (Leader Lessons 10, 11, 14). Every leader will have his or her time in the sun and the sun will surely set one day – only to rise again.

Now beloved you are obligated to share the rich lessons you learned with co-laborers and emerging leaders. The church is in the postmodern wilderness of the 21st Century. People want to get to their individual promised land and need support, guidance and encouragement. Our job is not to make promises but keep the promise entrusted to each one of us by God Almighty. It is not by personal power, individual might, but, as Moses discovered, the Spirit of the Lord that wrought great miracles.

The same Spirit that led the people out of bondage, helped conquer stronger enemies, fed, and then led by a cloud by day and pillar of fire by night, is the same Spirit that guides God's chosen and faithful leaders today. Beloved, my hope is that you will work the numbers like never before because you surely do count. We started this book with a blessing and we will close with the same.

The Lord bless you and keep you; the Lord make his face shine upon you and be gracious to you; the Lord turn his face toward you and give you peace...

Afterword

*By Reverend Dr. Emma Jordan Simpson, Executive
Pastor, The Concord Baptist Church of Christ*

I was delighted when my mentor Alfonso Wyatt
asked me to read a few advance chapters of *Leadership
by Numbers*. I do not even remember when I first met
"Rev." I just know that whenever we met, he pulled
me under his wing right along with so many other
young leaders I know. My professional leadership
experiences have been in church and community. I
have served as executive vice president for a
community development corporation; led the launch
of a local affiliate of a national gender equity
organization; led a statewide child advocacy
organization; and, served as interim leader of a major
human services organization. I now serve as executive
pastor of a large, urban, historic Baptist congregation.
In each setting, I have called upon Rev. Wyatt who
has the very special gift of reminding leaders about
why we serve.

One occasion in particular still holds deep meaning
for me. I was facing a particular leadership challenge
and was feeling a bit insecure because of the
pushback I was getting from my board over a
decision I made. I know that my decision was the
right one. I did not know how to interpret my board's
resistance. I called Reverend Wyatt, not particularly
wanting to talk about the challenge I was facing, but
rather just to hear his voice and laughter. I wanted
him to tell me one of his crazy stories or hit me with
one of his rhymes. True to who he is, however, once

he heard my voice he ended our call with "quick grace" and then showed up at my office in person 30 minutes later. I did not ask him to come.

He was invested enough in me as a young leader to make me a priority in that moment. I know the professional responsibility he was carrying himself. Yet, there he was in my office asking me about what was important to me as a leader and reminding me that I was enough. I will always remember what that meant to me as a young leader. I cannot preach like him and no one endeavors to mimic his charisma. There is only one Rev! I have tried to replicate for my staff and the people I have mentored the discipline of investing in a leader. It looks like showing up in a person's struggle and being present with people who were facing challenges. The gift is not in the answers, but in the safe space to ask questions and uncover the layers of the principles that guide our leadership.

Reading his chapter on "Effective Leaders Know When to Follow" (Numbers 10:29-31), I was reminded of how our congregation has valued the gifts of young pastors who had come to our congregation to "follow" us. Because of my senior pastor's work and reputation as a mentor to pastors, my congregation was sought out by Lilly Endowment to create a Transition Into Ministry Program. While we have had many student ministers and interns over the years, this program is an intentional residential immersion experience.

Lilly Endowment Inc. began this initiative in 1999 to help American congregations address some of the challenges that new pastors experienced as they transitioned from "seminary student to full-time pastor." They noted with alarm the numbers of pastors who leave their churches and, sometimes, the ministry altogether within the first five years of graduating from seminary. Denominational leaders articulated this alarm across the spectrum. Why? There were plenty of reasons, but mostly because young pastors were not experiencing the kind of mentoring and support that every leader needs in order to be healthy and to lead with strength. Too often, we look at iconic leaders and wrongly assume that effectiveness equals charisma. Many assume that healthy leadership is synonymous with charisma. For the church, that translates into the ways that many congregations have called and supported dynamic preachers to be their pastors – when they were really not pastors. They were dynamic preachers. There is a difference. A healthy pastor must have gifts and skills beyond preaching.

We know that many young pastors across denominations were isolated in their first call congregations (professionally, geographically, etc.) and did not have the support to create or participate in safe spaces where they could express vulnerability or reflect on their growing "pastoral identity" in healthy ways. In many black church traditions and denominations, pastors find spaces to talk about preaching. There are preaching conferences, books and local meetings for fellowship. There are few, if any, efforts to support the mental and emotional health of pastors. There are few spiritual accountability peer groups. New pastors do not find many spaces to talk about the tough transitional issues. They do not gain access to the established networks of older pastors who might be emotionally available for mentoring.

Therefore, a significant number of young pastors were becoming frustrated as they experienced this isolation and that frustration propelled them to leave ministry and the church altogether in the first few years of service. Those who stayed through the isolation, who weathered the lonely formative years of their pastorates on their own, often developed unhealthy habits that undermined their effectiveness. They slipped into leadership styles and practices that were unable to sustain their ministries—styles and practices that were often detrimental to their congregations.

We began participating in Lilly Endowment's Transition into Ministry program because we wanted African American pastors to experience the kind of immersion, mentoring and practice/reflection space that would give them a good start into full time ministry. We wanted them to have a safe space to fail at a project, miss the mark in a sermon, miss the sick visitation and then learn how to recover within the context of a loving community. In addition, we wanted to share what we were learning with other congregations. Since this program started, we have "graduated" about twelve pastors who are now serving in congregations as staff pastors, leading as senior pastors, or in campus ministries. They are in new contexts, but our senior pastor often shows up wherever they are across the country to be present with them. Our congregation loves them fiercely and these leaders have had their leadership affirmed and confirmed.

We have expanded to collaborate with three other Baptist congregations conducting their own Pastoral Residency Program in our region. Over the years, we have tried to mentor, model and teach what we believe sustains long, vibrant, healthy pastorates:

- Becoming a "pastor" is a way of life, not a destination.

- Congregations form pastors; therefore healthy congregations are paramount.

- Pastoring is something we do among people, not to them.

- Pastors need pastors.

- Pastors need healthy relationships with peers.

Back to *Leadership By Numbers*, when I read this chapter "Effective Leaders Know When to Follow" (Numbers 10:29-32), I was reminded of how our congregation has valued the gifts our young resident pastors have brought to our congregation and what we have learned from them over the years. They came to us to learn what it means to be "pastor among people" – but we also learned so much when we followed their lead. We saw ministry through their eyes and we were blessed with new birth:

- One resident pastor carved out a space for "teen talk" that now reaches disconnected young people in our community that our church would probably never have reached through existing outreach. In her eyes, community youth who were often forgotten and overlooked needed us to prioritize a space for their own for their "talk" to be sacred.

- One resident pastor used the vigor of his body to pump up young people in our summer literacy and social justice program, setting a standard for engagement that everyone after must meet. In his eyes, young people needed the people who led them to "bring it 5,000% every morning, without fail" if they were going to trust us to teach them something that challenged the world they saw every day.

- One resident pastor had a gift for asking the most unusual questions about church administration. In his eyes, good and courageous questions would help us to be better stewards of the resources for the work of ministry.

The list goes on for the ways that our historic congregation found moments of renewal for ministry when we saw through the eyes of these young leaders who came to learn from us. Borrowing the eyes of young leaders is not easy. Eventually, young leaders take us places we would not go ourselves. They see things we know are there, but we do not want to see. They are comfortable camping in places that make us uncomfortable. However, that is the beauty of mentoring. It is give and take. It is mutual. We are all stretched and made new. And as Moses said to Hobab, the best part of walking with someone who is trying to follow God, "whatever good the Lord does for us, the same we will do for you" (Numbers 10:32 NRSV).

The Rev. Dr. Emma Jordan-Simpson is the Executive Pastor of The Concord Baptist Church of Christ, Brooklyn, NY. She is the sixth of seven children born to a single mother in Newark, New Jersey. She preached her first sermon at the age of 17 years old at House of Prayer Episcopal Church, in Newark. She attended public schools in Newark and graduated from Arts High School in 1981 before going on to Fisk University in Nashville, Tennessee as a "first-generation" college student. She graduated with honors in 1985 with a Bachelor of Arts degree with a double major—Religious and Philosophical Studies and Music. She graduated from Union Theological Seminary in New York City with a Master of Divinity degree in 1988. She earned the Certificate in Not for Profit Management, Executive Level from the Columbia Business School Institute for Not for Profit Management in 1995, and earned the Doctor of Ministry Degree (with distinction) from Drew Theological Seminary in 2009. She is married to the Rev. Dr. Gary V. Simpson, Senior Pastor of The Concord Baptist Church of Christ. They have three children, Candace Yonina, David Michael and Jordan Elizabeth.

Suggested Reading

Anderson, Neil. *Victory Over Darkness: Realizing Your Identity In Christ*

Baron, David. *Moses on Management: 50 Leadership Lessons from The Greatest Manager of All Time*

Beattie, Melody. *Co-Dependent No More: How to Stop Controlling Others and Start Caring for Yourself*

Belf-E, Teri. *Coaching With Spirit: Allowing Success to Emerge*

Bennis, Warren. *Why Leaders Can't Lead: The Unconscious Conspiracy Continues*

Brinckerhoff C. Peter. *Faith Based Management: leading Organizations That Are Based On More Than Just Mission*

Covey, R. Stephen. *Principle Centered Leadership*

Covey, R. Stephen. *The 7 Habits of Highly Effective People: Powerful Lessons in Personal Change*

Damazio, Frank. *The Making of A Leader: Biblical Leadership Principles for Today's Leaders*

Fisher, C. James & Kathleen M. Cole. *Leadership and Management of Volunteer Programs*

Foster, J. Richard. *Celebration of Discipline: The Path to Spiritual Growth*

Goleman, Daniel. *Emotional Intelligence: Why it can matter more than I Q*

Harbaugh, L. Gary. *God's Gifted People: Discovering Your Personality as a Gift*

Hesselbein, Frances, Marshall Goldsmith & Richard Beckhard. *The Drucker Foundation The Leader of The Future*

Kouzes, M. James & Barry Z. Posner. *Leadership Challenge*

MacAdam, Millard. *Intentional Integrity: Aligning Your Life with God's Values*

McIntosh, L. Gary & Samuel D. Rima Sr.. *Overcoming The Dark Side of Leadership: The Paradox of Personal Dysfunction*

Moore, Thomas. *Care of the Soul: A Guide for Cultivating Depth and Sacredness in Everyday Life*

Neenan, Michael & Windy Dryden. *Life Coaching: A Cognitive-Behavioural Approach*

Oswald, M. Roy & Otto Kroeger. *Personality Type and Religious Leadership*

Perkins, Bill. *Awaken The Leader Within: How the Wisdom of Jesus Can Unleash Your Potential*

Riso, R. Don. *Personality Types: Using The Enneagram For Self-Discovery*

Scazzero, Peter & Geri Scazzero. *Emotionally Healthy Spirituality*

Schaef, W. Anne & Diane Fassel. *The Addictive Organization: Why We Overwork, Cover Up, Pick Up the Pieces, Please the Boss & Perpetuate Sick Organizations*

Warren, Rick. *The Purpose Driven Life: What On Earth Am I Here For?*

Wilson D. Sandra. *Hurt people Hurt People: Hope & Healing For Yourself And Your Relationships*

Wyatt, Alfonso & Ouida Wyatt. *Soul Be Free Poems Prose & Prayers*

Wyatt, Alfonso & Ouida Wyatt. *Soul Be Free II*

Wyatt, Alfonso. *Mentoring From The Inside Out: Healing Boys Transforming Men*

Rev. Dr. Alfonso Wyatt is on the staff of The Greater Allen Cathedral A.M.E. Cathedral of New York. He provides vital leadership to youth, young adults and professionals in both the sacred and secular communities. He retired as vice president of The Fund for the City of New York after serving over two decades. Dr. Wyatt is founder of Strategic Destiny: Designing Futures Through Faith and Facts. Strategic Destiny  collaborates with practitioners motivated by faith and secular practitioners motivated by evidence-based learning. He is an advisor and consultant to government, colleges, civic groups, community based organizations, public and charter schools, education intermediaries, foundations and the broader faith community.

Dr. Wyatt has mentored thousands ranging from young people in foster care, juvenile detention facilities, adults in prison, as well as individuals in: corporate America, youth serving organizations, the faith community, or receiving their Ph.D. He is a sought after speaker in his role as youth development practitioner, mentor, role model and public theologian. He attended Howard University, Columbia Teachers College, The Ackerman Institute for Family Therapy, Columbia Institute for Nonprofit Management and New York Theological Seminary. Rev. Dr. Wyatt is a founding Board member of The Harlem Children's Zone Promise Academy. He also serves on the Boards of Interfaith Center of New York, Correctional & Osborne Associations, and served as Chair of The 21st Century Foundation, powered by Tides.

CPSIA information can be obtained
at www.ICGtesting.com
Printed in the USA
FFHW01n0423220918
48434819-52287FF